STORM
CLOUDS
ON THE
HORIZON

STORM CLOUDS
ON THE
HORIZON

**BIBLE PROPHECY AND THE
CURRENT MIDDLE EAST CRISIS**

CHARLES H. DYER

GENERAL EDITOR

MOODY PRESS
CHICAGO

This book is dedicated to the students and alumni of Moody Bible Institute who, for over a century, have faithfully served our Lord as they "wait for his Son from heaven, whom he raised from the dead —Jesus, who rescues us from the coming wrath" (1 Thess. 1:10).

God bless the school that D. L. Moody founded;
Firm may she stand, tho' by foes of truth surrounded!
Riches of grace bestowed may she never squander,
Keeping true to God and man her record over yonder.

CONTENTS
⋆

Each of the contributors to this volume currently serves on the faculty or administration at Moody Bible Institute.

ISRAEL MY GLORY
✳
Dr. Joseph M. Stowell

When I think of the nation Israel, I am tempted to think of Humpty Dumpty. This once proud nation that humbled the Egyptian Empire in a slave revolt that led to a supernaturally blessed exodus; that caused the greatest armies of the known world to quake; that became the repository of divine law in the midst of a pagan lawless world . . . today finds itself broken by international isolation and a seemingly insoluable conflict with its Palestinian neighbors. And all the king's horses and all the king's men of this world's peace-brokering intermediaries can't seem to put it all back together again.

This would be of little consequence if you didn't believe that God has a future for Israel. If the hand of God removed itself forever from His people when the Jews rejected Christ as Messiah, then Israel would be just another nation among many, stuck at the eastern end of the Mediterranean, surrounded and outnumbered by enemy states.

But if you are among the many who believe that God's promises to Israel were unconditional—and that He ultimately will redeem them to Himself and restore His glory among them —then Israel becomes *the* strategic player in the future history of this world. Especially when that belief encompasses the promise that Christ's return to this planet will be to the Mount of Olives just outside of Jerusalem and that He will establish His reign on the throne of David as the fulfillment of the covenant that God made with David that his throne would last forever. Given this promise, Israel becomes the focal point of the attention of all of us who love His appearing. And it raises the suspicion that, behind the headlines, the hand of our sovereign God is working to put the pieces back together again.

Throughout our long history, the Moody Bible Institute has been among those who see God's Word guaranteeing Israel's future. This belief has characterized and permeated our teaching . . . and has kept fresh our desire to see the salvation of His people. We are humbled to think that God in His extensive grace has grafted Gentiles in to the redemptive gifts of His Son and counted us among His very own. And this perspective has also kept our eyes focused heavenward as we wait expectantly for the rapture of His church . . . for we know that our summons home also signals the time when God will begin the consummation of His plan for His Chosen People Israel.

It is my prayer that this work, written by leading members of our faculty, will reignite your desire for His return, encourage your confidence in His eternal plan in the midst of confusing and despairing headlines, and stimulate a new love for the people that He loves. Read it prayerfully and hopefully, looking for God to stir your heart again to love His appearing.

ISRAEL: THE LINCHPIN IN GOD'S PROGRAM FOR THE FUTURE

✴

Dr. Michael Rydelnik

> *All things are mortal but the Jew; all other forces pass,*
> *but he remains. What is the secret of his immortality?*
> —MARK TWAIN

Perhaps you have heard of Mr. Goldstein who was said to have made a visit to heaven as the representative of the Jewish people. He met the Lord and asked, "Is it true that we are the Chosen People?" The Lord boomed His response: "Yes, it's true, you are the Chosen People." To which Mr. Goldstein replied, "Would You mind choosing somebody else for a change!" This joke, which is often told by Jewish people, reflects the terrible history of Jewish suffering that has made some Jewish people view God's choice as a burden. However, being God's Chosen People is a great privilege that God in His mercy has bestowed upon His people, placing them squarely in the center of history and prophecy.

How is it that this small group of people has had such an immense impact on society? The Jewish people comprise only one-half of 1 percent of the world's population, yet win 20 percent of the Nobel Prizes that are awarded. The entire world recognizes the achievements of Jewish notables such as Jonas Salk who developed the polio vaccine, Albert Einstein whose theory of relativity catapulted the world into the Atomic Age, and Sigmund Freud who was the father of psychotherapy. People ask why the small State of Israel, which is about the size of the state of New Jersey, seems to have such a large role in world events, with global coverage of its daily activities.

Certainly Jewish people have had—and will continue to have—a profound influence on the world because of God's choice of Israel to be His people. By examining God's Word, it is possible to understand what is happening in the news today and what will take place in the future. The best place to start doing that is by looking at the past—when God first called Israel to be His Chosen People.

ISRAEL'S PAST

The unconditional covenants that God made with Israel in the past are foundational for understanding Israel's importance in the prophetic future. These covenants with Israel govern our understanding of the Jewish people and form the backbone of Bible prophecy.

The Abrahamic Covenant

Genesis 12:1–3 records God's call of Abraham out of Ur of the Chaldees (Babylon) and the specific promises He made to him. These promises were confirmed and clarified in later passages of Genesis (13:14–17; 15:1–7; 17:1–21). Additionally, they were reconfirmed to Abraham's son Isaac (26:3–4) and grandson Jacob (28:13–15), specifying which line of Abraham would receive God's promises.

The promises God made to Abraham fall into three categories: personal, national, and universal. The *personal* promises God gave to Abraham included a great name, vast wealth, and abundant spiritual blessing for himself. The life of Abraham as recorded in Scripture confirms that these promises were fulfilled.

God added the *national* promise that Abraham's descendants would multiply and be "as numerous as the stars in the sky and as the sand on the seashore" (22:17). Additionally, God promised Abraham that He would give the nation of Israel the land of Canaan as their "everlasting possession" (17:8) with its boundaries extending from the river of Egypt in the West to the Euphrates River in the East, and to the land of the Hittites in the North (15:18–21). This is interesting in light of all the contemporary questions about ownership of the land of Israel today. Regardless of the political disputes, God has granted the title deed of the land of Israel to the Jewish people. Furthermore, this land promise was never fulfilled in its entirety. Since God always keeps His promises, it is certain that one day, in the Messianic Kingdom, Israel will dwell in all the land that God promised.

The national promises also gave Israel a unique position as God's barometer of blessing—those nations that would bless Israel would be blessed and those that cursed Israel would be cursed (12:3; 27:29). This principle applied in the life of Abraham (12:10–20; 14:12–20; 26:1–11) and throughout the history of the Jewish people (Deut. 30:7; Isa. 14:1–2). Significantly, this will be the principle that guides God's judgment of the Gentile nations when Jesus returns. In Jesus' parable of the sheep and the goats, which represent the judgment of the Gentiles, the nations will be divided on the basis of their treatment of Jesus' physical brethren, the Jewish people. That is why Jesus will say, "Whatever you did for one of the least of these brothers of mine, you did for me" (Matt. 25:40).

Regarding the *universal* aspects of the Abrahamic Covenant, God promised to bless the whole world through Abraham (Gen. 12:3) and specifically through his "offspring," that is, his future descendants (22:18). The ultimate fulfillment of this promise was found when Jesus, the Messiah of Israel, provided atonement for the whole world through His death and resurrection (Gal. 3:16).

The Other Covenants

The Land Covenant. Later biblical covenants expanded three particular aspects of the Abrahamic Covenant, namely the promises of the land, the seed, and the blessing. The land promise was expanded into the Land Covenant found in Deuteronomy 28–30. This promise assured that Israel would experience physical and material blessing from God if they would obey His law. However, God also threatened to discipline the nation for persistent disobedience and idolatry by driving the people out of the land and into exile. Finally, God promised to restore the Jewish people to their land after much suffering. God states that both their suffering and their restoration will occur "in [the] later days" (Deut. 4:30; 31:29).

The Davidic Covenant. God's promise of seed for Abraham was further expanded in the Davidic Covenant. This covenant is foundational for the messianic hope of the Hebrew Bible and the basis of the New Testament expectation of a future kingdom. Though David wanted to build a house (temple) for God, God instead promised to build a house (dynasty) for David (2 Sam. 7:11). God affirmed that He would give David an eternal dynasty and kingdom with an eternal Ruler to sit on David's throne (v. 16). That Ruler was to be one of David's sons (his seed) who was also to have a Father/Son relationship with God (vv. 12–16).

In the course of the historical narrative of 1 Kings, it appears that this promise would be fulfilled through Solomon. In fact, since Solomon even believed that he was the potential fulfillment, he built the temple. But the Lord warned Solomon that the promise would be fulfilled through him only if he would "follow my decrees, carry out my regulations and keep all my commands" (1 Kings 6:12). The author of 1 Kings quickly points out how miserably Solomon failed because of his marriages to foreign women who turned his heart away from God (11:1–4). In fact, no Davidic king succeeded in obeying God completely. All of them, even the good ones, ended with failure. Thus the book of 2 Kings ends with the hope and expectation that God will one day send an eternal Ruler who will build the true temple of God and sit on the throne of David. The prophet Zechariah foretold that this future King will come to unite the offices of Priest and King and build the temple of the Lord (Zech. 6:9–15).

The hope and longing for this Son of David consumed the prophets (Isa. 11:1, 10; 16:5; Jer. 23:5; 30:9; 33:15–17; Ezek.

34:23–24; 37:24–28; Hos. 3:4–5; Amos 9:11–15) and found its fulfillment in the birth of Jesus. The angel Gabriel announced His birth, saying, "The Lord God will give him the throne of his father David, and he will reign over the house of Jacob forever; his kingdom will never end" (Luke 1:32–33). Jesus was the Promised One, the Son of David and the Son of God. He announced the coming of God's kingdom, and He will return to rule from the literal throne of David in Jerusalem and establish the kingdom of God on earth.

The New Covenant. The blessing component of the Abrahamic Covenant was amplified by the New Covenant. The name "New Covenant" comes from Jeremiah 31:31–34, but it had already been promised in the Pentateuch (Deut. 30:1–14) and would be affirmed in other prophets (Ezek. 36:26–27). The newness of this covenant is derived from its distinction from the Old Covenant, the Mosaic Law. In Jeremiah 31:32 the New Covenant is said to be unlike the Old Covenant God gave Israel when the nation left Egypt. This Old Covenant is an obvious reference to the Mosaic Law, not the Abrahamic Covenant or any other covenant. Hebrews 8:13 confirms this when it states that the Old Covenant (Mosaic Law) has been made obsolete by the establishment of the New Covenant.

The New Covenant was promised to Israel and Judah and was ratified through the death of Jesus on the cross (Matt. 26:27–28; Luke 22:20). Today, the church shares those spiritual blessings through its relationship with the Messiah Jesus. However, only when Messiah returns and begins His kingdom will He establish the New Covenant in its fullest sense. In that day, when everyone knows the Lord, all people will fully experience this universal aspect of the Abrahamic Covenant.

Since God keeps His promises, these covenants from Israel's past remain significant for her present and future. The land aspect of the Abrahamic Covenant reaffirms that the title deed to the land of Israel belongs to the Jewish people. Israel never fully possessed the land as described in the Abrahamic Covenant. Even at the zenith of David's and Solomon's rule, the land they governed did not match the land grant God gave Abraham. Therefore, the covenant assures that there will be a future kingdom which will include all the land God promised—something which, throughout her long history, Israel has never possessed. The Davidic Covenant assures that Jesus the Messiah, the Son of David, will return and establish His kingdom on earth. He will rule from David's throne as the righteous King of Israel and Sovereign of the world. Finally, the New Covenant guarantees that there will be a time when all Israel will turn to her Messiah. Then Israel and all the nations of the world will know the Lord. These covenants certainly give hope for the future . . . but what of Israel today? We now turn to Israel's present.

ISRAEL'S PRESENT

Since these covenants are all from Israel's past, some have improperly taken them away from Israel and applied them to the church today. It is true that the vast majority of Jewish people have failed to recognize Jesus as their Messiah. This rejection has motivated some sincere followers of Christ to adopt the erroneous opinion that Israel's promises have transferred to the church. Their approach seems to take a rather shortsighted view of the faithfulness of God.

One of the essential principles of the Abrahamic Covenant was that it was unconditional and eternal. Abraham did not need to do anything to receive or maintain this covenant. Furthermore, when God reaffirmed His covenant with Abraham, He solemnized His divine oath with the offering of sacrifices (Gen. 15:9–17). In ancient times, when two parties wanted to bind themselves to a covenant, they would lay the severed parts of a sacrificial animal on the ground and both parties would walk in their midst. This signified that both were in agreement and bound by the covenant. When God solemnized His oath to Abraham, He deliberately excluded Abraham from the process. Instead, God caused Abraham to fall into a deep sleep, and God alone passed through the animal parts. This demonstrated that God was solely responsible for this covenant—it did not depend on Abraham or his descendants but on God alone. In light of the unconditional nature of the Abrahamic Covenant, there are several truths about the Jewish people today that must be maintained.

God Has Retained Israel as His Chosen People

This is not only an Old Testament concept; the New Testament agrees with it as well. Paul writes that, despite Israel's disbelief in Jesus, God did not reject His people whom He foreknew (Rom. 11:1–2). Moreover, Paul adds that although most Jewish people have rejected the good news of Jesus, the people of Israel remain God's beloved Chosen People "on account of the patriarchs" (v. 28)—a clear reference to the Abrahamic Covenant. Paul categorically states that God's gifts and call to Israel are irrevocable (v. 29).

Remaining God's Chosen People does not mean that Jewish people have forgiveness and a personal relationship with God apart from faith in their Messiah Jesus. Jewish people, as all people, must trust in Jesus. Regardless, the Lord's words in Deuteronomy 14:2 remain as true as ever. "Out of all the peoples on the face of the earth, the LORD has chosen you to be his treasured possession." God did this not because of any merit found in the Jewish people. Rather, He chose them, as Moses wrote earlier in Deuteronomy, "because the LORD loved you and kept the oath he swore to your forefathers" (7:8). Since God is faithful to His promises and loyal in His love, the Jewish people are still the Chosen People.

God Is Active Today Preserving and Protecting the Jewish People

The Lord, through the prophet Jeremiah, assures us that it will be impossible ever to destroy the Jewish people. In fact, in order to put an end to the Jewish people, it would be necessary to stop the sun, moon, and stars from shining and also to measure all the heavens and the foundations of the earth. God declares that only if these impossible acts could be accomplished will "the descendants of Israel ever cease to be a nation before me" or "will I reject all the descendants of Israel" (Jer. 31:35–37). Plainly, the Lord will preserve His people. That is why the prophet Zechariah says of the people of Israel that whoever touches them "touches the apple of his [God's] eye" (Zech. 2:8).

Throughout history, there have been those who have sought Israel's destruction—from Haman to Hitler to Saddam Hussein—but they have never succeeded. In 1981 I attended the World Gathering of Holocaust Survivors in Jerusalem, as a second-generation participant. There I heard Menachem Begin, the late prime minister of Israel, declare before those Holocaust survivors and their children that Hitler's attempt to annihilate the Jewish people ought not to cause them to doubt God's existence but rather to believe in Him. Begin said that apart from God's providential intervention there was no way Hitler could have failed. The prime minister recognized that God was true to His promise to preserve and ultimately to protect His Chosen People. Frederick the Great was said to have asked his chaplain for one clear and compelling evidence for the existence of God. The chaplain replied, "The amazing Jew, Your Majesty."

The preservation of the Jewish people, despite a history of hatred and persecution, has led historian Paul Johnson to call the Jews "the most tenacious people in history." It is far better to say that the Jewish people are protected by the tenacious God of history, who is faithful to His promises and relentless in preserving His people. For this reason, no weapon formed against Israel will ever prevail (Isa. 54:17).

God Is Presently Saving a Remnant of Israel

Paul asserted, in Romans 11:1–5, that God did not reject the Jewish people; and as proof he offered the doctrine of the remnant. His point was that God has always worked through a faithful remnant both during the Old Testament and in the present age. Even though the vast majority of the Jewish people have rejected Jesus as the Messiah, God in His faithfulness has preserved a remnant within Israel, chosen by grace, who would believe. Paul writes, "So too, at the present time there is a remnant chosen by grace" (v. 5).

Throughout the entire church age, there has always been a remnant of Jewish people who have sincerely believed in Jesus as their Messiah and Lord. Since 1967 a significant number of Jewish people have come to believe in Jesus and still maintain their unique role as the Jewish remnant. There are approximately

250,000 Messianic Jews worldwide participating in hundreds of Messianic congregations and in many evangelical churches. This movement is also evident in Europe, South America, the former Soviet Union, and Israel.

Paul anticipated a day when the remnant would become the whole. He writes in Romans 11:25–26 that at Jesus' return, when the full number of Gentiles have come in, Israel as a whole will turn to Jesus in faith as their Messiah and so "all Israel will be saved." Perhaps the Spirit of God's unique move among the Jewish people today is but a precursor to the far greater movement that will take place yet in the future.

God Is Restoring the Jewish People to the Land of Israel

Since their exile around the world nearly two millennia ago, Jewish people have daily prayed that they would be restored to the land of Israel. The Hebrew prophets foretold a day when God would draw His people back to their promised land. Throughout church history Christians, for the most part, could not conceive of a literal fulfillment of this promise, so they interpreted it figuratively. However, some believers in the nineteenth century did indeed take the promise of a return literally and therefore began to anticipate a Jewish return to the land of Israel.

In the last part of the nineteenth century, Jewish groups arose in eastern Europe, known as the "Lovers of Zion." They believed that a return to the land of Israel was the only hope for Jewish people to survive in a world filled with anti-Jewish hatred. In 1881 the very first Jewish people began to return to build a homeland. This first immigration wave, known in Hebrew as an *aliyah* (literally "ascent"), was difficult and did not see much success.

By 1894, Theodor Herzl, a Viennese journalist and an assimilated Jew, was covering the treason trial of the French Jewish Captain Alfred Dreyfus. It was apparent that Dreyfus was innocent but falsely accused solely because he was Jewish. Crowds roamed the streets of Paris, crying, "Death to the Jews." That this could occur in liberal France, the seat of Jewish emancipation and freedom, devastated and transformed Herzl. He wrote *The Jewish State* which called for the return of the Jewish people to their historic homeland as the only solution to anti-Semitism. Herzl formed the World Zionist Organization and convened the First Zionist Congress in Basel, Switzerland, in 1897. There he wrote in his journal, "In Basel, I founded the Jewish state!" He anticipated that within fifty years there would be a revived Jewish state in what was then known as Palestine. This sparked a second wave of Jewish immigration from eastern Europe, which included David Ben-Gurion (Israel's first prime minister) and Yitzchak Ben-Zvi (Israel's second president), to *Eretz Yisrael* (the land of Israel).

The next major development occurred during World War I. For a variety of reasons, the British Empire through its foreign secretary, Arthur Balfour, issued "The Balfour Declaration." This private letter to the Jewish Lord Rothschild declared that "His Majesty's Government view with favour the establishment in Palestine of a national home for the Jewish people, and will use their best endeavours to facilitate the achievement of this object. . . ." After the war, this declaration was accepted by the League of Nations, which granted the British the mandate for Palestine in order for them to carry out Balfour's declaration.

Many in Great Britain and around the world saw the regathering as the beginnings of prophecy being fulfilled, including

Balfour himself. As Jewish people returned to their ancient homeland, they found support among Bible-believing Christians. By 1923, in support of the return of Jewish people to their land and seeing the need for end-time missionaries to the Jewish people, the Moody Bible Institute established a Jewish Studies program.

Despite shifts in British policy, particularly during World War II, vast numbers of Jewish people returned to the land. In 1947 the United Nations partitioned Palestine between the Arab and the Jewish populations. The Jewish state was declared on May 14, 1948, with the end of the British mandate. The fledgling state was immediately attacked by all the surrounding Arab nations. Against all odds Israel survived; and in 1967 the nation fought, and won, the dramatic Six-Day War which saw the reunification of Jerusalem.

Bible believers frequently ask how the unprecedented, reborn State of Israel fits with Bible prophecy. For several reasons, it appears that the best explanation is that the modern State of Israel seems to be a dramatic work of God in fulfillment of the Bible's predictions of a Jewish return to the land of Israel.

First, the Bible predicts that Israel will return to her land in unbelief. Biblical prophecy indicates that the Jewish people will turn to God only *after* returning to the land of Israel. Ezekiel 36:24 states, "For I will take you out of the nations; I will gather you from all the countries and bring you back into your own land." The next two verses continue, "I will sprinkle clean water on you, and you will be clean; I will cleanse you from all your impurities and from all your idols. I will give you a new heart and put a new spirit in you; I will remove from you your heart of stone and give you a heart of flesh." Note that the *national* restoration of the Jewish people will precede the *spiritual* regeneration of Israel. Israel has been reborn as a secular state by secular Jews. This is the precursor of the day when the entire nation turns in faith to the Messiah Jesus.

Second, the Bible predicts that Israel will return to her land in stages. Ezekiel 37 contains the vision of a valley of dry bones. The bones come to life in stages, first, sinews on the bones, then flesh, then skin, and finally, the breath of life (vv. 6–10). Then God tells Ezekiel that "these bones are the whole house of Israel" (v. 11) and that their restoration is a picture of the way God will bring them "back to the land of Israel" (v. 12). So the regathering of Israel is not an event that will occur in one fell swoop. Rather, it is a process that culminates in the nation's receiving the breath of life by turning to their Messiah. This is precisely how the Jewish people have returned to the land. Through the different waves of immigration, from the first in 1881 to the most recent wave of immigrants from the former Soviet Union, the Jewish people have returned in stages. The final step will be when the entire nation turns in faith to Jesus their Messiah, and God breathes the breath of life on them.

Third, the Bible predicts that Israel will return to her land through persecution. God says of Israel through the prophet Jeremiah, "I will restore them to the land I gave their forefathers" (16:15). In the next verse, God says that He will use "fishermen" and "hunters" to pursue His people back to their land (v. 16). This metaphor for persecution has been literally fulfilled. Since the birth of modern Zionism, the primary motivation for return to the land of Israel has been anti-Jewish persecution. In the last 100 years, God has used czarist pogroms, Polish economic discrimination, Nazi genocide, Arab hatred, and Soviet repression to drive Jewish people back to their homeland. Economic success and religious freedom in the Diaspora keep Jewish people complacent about returning; so God uses "fishermen" and "hunters" to drive them back to the Promised Land.

Fourth, the Bible predicts that Israel will return to her land to set the stage for end-time events. Daniel 9:27 speaks of a firm covenant between the future world dictator and the Jewish people which will unleash the final events before Messiah Jesus' return. This prophecy assumes a reborn State of Israel. The Jewish state had to be restored so this prediction (and many others) can take place. There needs to be a reborn State of Israel for this treaty to be signed, for the temple to be rebuilt, for Jerusalem to be surrounded by the nations during the campaign of Armageddon, and for Jesus to return to deliver the Jewish people from their enemies. Since Israel has returned in unbelief, in stages, and through persecution, it is likely that the modern State of Israel fulfills the predictions of the ancient Hebrew prophets . . . and sets the stage for events yet to come.

God established His plan for Israel in the ancient past by establishing His covenants with the Jewish people. On the basis of these covenants, God continues to work among the Jewish people in the present age. But God has much more in store for Israel in the future. In fact, He has given the Jewish people a featured role to play in the outworking of end-time events.

ISRAEL'S FUTURE

Throughout history, God has caused the Jewish people to have an influence that far outweighs their size. This will be even more true in the future. In examining the end times, there are several ways in which Israel will be the focal point in God's future program.

Israel Will Play a Vital Role in Starting the Future Tribulation

Although the Bible teaches that Jesus can return for His church at any moment (Matt. 25:1–13; 1 Thess. 5:2–6), it gives a specific requirement for the beginning of the future Tribulation period. The Tribulation will begin only when Israel signs a covenant (a treaty of some sort) with the future false Messiah. According to Daniel 9:27, the seventieth "seven" of Daniel's vision begins when "he will confirm a covenant with many for one 'seven.'" The identity of the "he" in this verse is a future world ruler who will set up an abomination in a yet-to-be-built temple. This ruler is frequently called "the Antichrist" or the "man of sin," but I prefer to call him the future "false messiah."

This false messiah makes a covenant or treaty with *many*. From the context, it appears that the *many* refers either to many in Israel or to Israel and her neighbors. This treaty, either between Israel and the false messiah or Israel and her neighbors but brokered by the false messiah, will most likely establish peace in the Middle East for the first half of the Tribulation (three and a half years). But the false messiah will then break the covenant and unleash hell on earth, culminating in the campaign of Armageddon.

The point is this: The Messiah Jesus can return for the church at any time—even as you read this paragraph. But the Tribulation will only begin when Israel and the future false messiah make a treaty together—showing Israel's vital role as a catalyst for the Tribulation period. Besides starting the Tribulation, Israel is crucial for other aspects of future events.

Israel Will Be the Focus of the Tribulation

The prophet Jeremiah clarifies this when he calls the Tribulation period "a time of trouble *for Jacob*" (Jer. 30:7, italics added). The name "Jacob" refers in this context not to the patriarch but the people that descended from him. Israel is God's primary concern during the Tribulation since the church will have already been removed at the Rapture. Israel's central place in the Tribulation is evident in several ways.

First, the Tribulation will be a time of Israel's *persecution*. In Revelation 12, God describes Satan's activity at both the Messiah's first coming and at His second coming. He uses the figure of "a woman clothed with the sun, with the moon under her feet and a crown of twelve stars on her head" (v. 1). In light of Joseph's dream (Gen. 37:9), it is best to understand the woman as a reference to Israel. The woman (Israel) gave birth to a Son (Jesus, the Messianic King), who was persecuted by the dragon (Satan) at the time of His birth (Rev. 12:1–6). This happened at Jesus' first coming through the attempt by Herod the Great to destroy the rightful King of the Jewish people (Matt. 2:13–18).

Prior to the second coming of the Messiah, the Dragon will be cast to the earth and will begin to persecute "the woman who had given birth to the male child" (Rev. 12:13), namely, Israel. Not only will the Dragon be "enraged at the woman" (Israel) but he will make war "against the rest of her offspring" (v. 17). This refers to the future satanic attacks on both the nation and the remnant of Israel who will come to faith during the Tribulation. It will be a time of unprecedented hatred and persecution of Jewish people.

Second, the Tribulation will be a time of Israel's *cleansing*. God will permit the suffering of His Chosen People in order to discipline them so that they will turn in faith to Jesus and accept Him as their Messiah. The prophet Ezekiel speaks of the Tribulation as the time when Israel passes under God's rod of discipline (Ezek. 20:37). This discipline will result in Israel's being purged of rebels (those who have not yet trusted in Jesus as their Messiah) while the rest of the nation will be brought into the bond of the covenant (vv. 37–38). The prophet Jeremiah records God's purpose for the Tribulation when God says to Israel, "I will discipline you but only with justice" (Jer. 30:11). According to Zechariah 13:9, God will discipline Israel in order to "refine them like silver and test them like gold." As a result, Israel will call on God's name and He will answer them. God will say, "'They are my people,' and they will say, 'The LORD is our God.'" God will use the suffering of the Jewish people to discipline them so that they will come to know the Lord through Jesus their Messiah.

Third, the Tribulation will be a time of Israel's *service*. During the Tribulation there will be 144,000 Jewish people, from the twelve tribes, who will be called "the servants of our God" (Rev. 7:3). They are Jewish people who come to faith in Jesus after the removal of the church at the Rapture. No doubt there will be Bibles and other materials that will enable the 144,000 to understand and receive the gospel. This remnant of Israel will be sealed by God and set apart for His service. What they will do in service to God is unclear. Perhaps they will be the evangelists of the Tribulation period, helping people all over the world put their trust in Jesus the Messiah, even during the Tribulation.

Fourth, the Tribulation will be a time of Israel's *war*. At the culmination of the Tribulation, world leaders will gather their armies in northern Israel, next to the hill of Megiddo, to begin the campaign of Armageddon (Rev. 16:16). These nations will march on Jerusalem and besiege the Jewish people there (Zech. 12:3). The attacking armies of the world will fight against Jerusalem, capture and ransack the city, and commit horrible atrocities (Zech. 14:2). God will allow this so that Israel will turn to Him and then be saved. The Tribulation will be a time of war for the Jewish people.

God's wrath will fall on the earth during the Tribulation period. It will be a time of suffering for all peoples. But more than any other nation, God will focus His attention on the Jewish people, with the goal of bringing them to faith in Jesus and restoring them to Himself. Besides Israel's importance in starting and being the focus of the Tribulation, the nation will play an even more significant role in the second coming of Jesus the Messiah.

Israel Will Initiate the Second Coming of the Messiah

Although no one knows the day or hour of Jesus' return for His church, we do know that He will return to earth at the conclusion of the seven-year Tribulation period. What will bring about the end of that period and the return of Messiah to the earth? The Scriptures teach that it will be Israel who will call for Jesus to return . . . and He will do so in His mercy.

Matthew 23:37–39 contains Jesus' response to Israel's national rejection of Him. There He says that He would have longed to gather Israel as a mother hen gathers her chicks. However, when the leadership of Israel rejected Jesus, they made such a gathering impossible. As a result, Jesus announced that Jerusalem and the temple would be destroyed. But He does offer Israel hope in the midst of this judgment. "For I tell you,

you will not see me again until you say, 'Blessed is he who comes in the name of the Lord'" (v. 39). Jesus requires Israel to say the traditional Hebrew words of welcome and reception. In effect, Jesus is saying that He will not return to Israel until they welcome Him as their Messiah. What will cause Israel to do this?

The prophet Zechariah predicted that at the end of the Tribulation the nations will gather in Israel and attack Jerusalem (Zech. 12:1–9). The suffering will have been so severe and the situation so grave that Israel's leaders will turn to their God for deliverance. God will then graciously open their eyes so that "They will look [in faith] on me, the one they have pierced, and they will mourn for him as one mourns for an only child, and grieve bitterly for him as one grieves for a firstborn son" (v. 10). Israel will mourn for all the years that they had rejected Jesus. Nevertheless, they will now welcome Him as their Messiah, saying, "Blessed is he who comes in the name of the Lord." The Messiah will return, and "a fountain will be opened . . . to cleanse them from sin and impurity" (13:1). Then, as Paul had foretold, all the Jewish people alive in that day will put their faith in Jesus as their Messiah. "And so all Israel will be saved" (Rom. 11:26).

Not only will the Lord deliver the Jewish people from their sin, He will also deliver them from their attackers. According to Zechariah, "Then the LORD will go out and fight against those nations, as he fights in the day of battle. On that day his feet will stand on the Mount of Olives. . . . Then the LORD my God will come, and all the holy ones with him" (Zech. 14:3–5). It is only when Israel calls for Jesus to return, and looks to Him in faith, that the Messiah will return. Israel is the key to the second coming of Christ. Even after Jesus returns, Israel will still have a crucial position in God's program.

Israel Will Be the Head of the Nations in the Messianic Kingdom

The Messianic Kingdom that Jesus will establish will have many marvelous components. From the renovation of the earth to universal peace, it will be a glorious time. But for Israel it will be especially remarkable. All the Jewish people will have turned to Jesus whom they will now know as Lord. Those who are still scattered around the world will be returned to the land of Israel and will fully inhabit the land according to the provisions of the Abrahamic Covenant.

The Messiah will begin His reign from the throne of David in Jerusalem and will rule over Israel and all the nations. Significantly, Israel will be the head of the nations then, even as the book of Deuteronomy had foretold. "The LORD will make you the head, not the tail" (28:13). Isaiah promised that God would again choose Israel and settle them in their land. Then "the house of Israel will possess the nations" (14:1–2).

Although many biblical passages speak of Israel's leadership of the Gentile nations in the Messianic kingdom (Isa. 49:22–23; 60:1–3; 61:4–9; Mic. 7:14–17; Zeph. 3:20), one is especially notable in that it speaks of the spiritual influence Israel will have over the nations. The Lord Almighty Himself describes the scene when many peoples and powerful nations will come to worship Him in Jerusalem. "In those days ten men from all languages and nations will take firm hold of one Jew by the hem of his robe and say, 'Let us go with you, because we have heard that God is with you'" (Zech. 8:23). When the Jewish people know the Lord, He will make them great and they will lead the

Gentile nations in worship of Him. This small nation of Israel will continue to have a large influence, even in the Messianic Kingdom. The ancient rabbis were right when they said, "Israel is like a vine: trodden underfoot; but some time later its wine is placed on the table of a king. So, Israel, at first oppressed, will eventually come to greatness" (Talmud: *Nedarim* 49b).

CONCLUSION

This chapter began with a quote from Mark Twain. "All things are mortal but the Jew; all other forces pass, but he remains. What is the secret of his immortality?" Twain has asked the right question. What is the secret of this special people? At the outset of this chapter, we asked the same question. The answer, as we have seen, lies in the Abrahamic Covenant. Long ago, God in His grace chose Israel to be His special people. Even in the present age, Israel remains God's Chosen People, the special object of His love and concern. Since this is true, God will be faithful to all the promises that He made to Abraham, Isaac, and Jacob. Therefore Israel remains the linchpin to biblical history and prophecy. God will continue to work among the Jewish people in order to bring them to faith in their Messiah and, ultimately, to place them at the head of the nations under the leadership of their Jewish King, Jesus, the Messianic Son of David.

THE CHURCH: WATCHING FOR OUR "BLESSED HOPE"

✳

Dr. Louis A. Barbieri

> *I will build my church,*
> *and the gates of Hades will not overcome it.*
> —MATTHEW 16:18

My son drove his Dodge Caravan into a parking place in the church parking lot and turned off the ignition switch. As his wife, Tamra, helped their twin daughters get out of their seat belts, Jeff walked around the van to get his almost-three-year-old son, Jake, out of his car seat. He opened the door and began to unbuckle Jake's seat belt, when much to his surprise Jake looked up at his dad and in a whiney voice said, "Dad, why do we always keep coming to church?"

As Jeff related this incident to us, he said that he almost had to laugh out loud, because he had sometimes wondered that very same thing. Some of us find ourselves at church every time the doors are opened while others never darken the doors of a church, unless it is to attend a wedding or a funeral. What is the church, why is it significant in the twenty-first century . . . and what is its future?

THE CHURCH VERSUS ISRAEL

In Matthew 16:18 Jesus announced to His disciples that He was going to be building His church. His use of the future tense ("will build") implies that the building of the church was something Jesus would be initiating in the future. While God's program for the church was clearly in His mind from all eternity, the church has a specific beginning point and ending point in history. One must understand the distinction between God's program for the church and His program for Israel to grasp properly His plan for the future.

God's Work with Israel

God's program for Israel began with His call of Abraham, originally named Abram. When He first revealed Himself to Abraham, God promised that his descendants would become a great nation (Gen. 12:2). This was a significant promise because Abraham and his wife had not been able to have children. Second, God promised that the descendants of Abraham would possess a land (12:7; 13:14–15; 15:18–19). Third, God stated that through Abraham all of the peoples of the earth would be blessed (12:3). These individual, national, and universal promises were confirmed forever when God entered into a blood covenant with Abraham, promising to do all that He had revealed (15:9–21). The remainder of the Old Testament details God's relationship to Israel . . . Abraham's descendants through the promised child, Isaac.

When Jesus came into the world, it was no accident that He came to the nation of Israel. As the promised Messiah, He came preaching that the kingdom had come near. If the nation would acknowledge Him as their Messiah King, God's promised kingdom would be established. Sadly, the people rejected their Messiah. Jesus was betrayed and crucified.

God's Work with the Church

With His death, resurrection, and ascension back to heaven, Jesus Christ was able to begin a new work among men, the building of His church. In His postresurrection ministry Jesus also told His disciples that they were going to experience a brand-new work of the Spirit. It is clear that the disciples did not understand what Jesus was saying, for their very next question for Him was "Lord, are you at this time going to restore the kingdom to Israel?" (Acts 1:6). They were still thinking about God's promises to the nation Israel and hoping they would have the privilege of seeing the Messianic Kingdom instituted immediately on the earth.

Jesus' answer to their question seems to remove any doubt about the future certainty of God's promised kingdom for Israel. If they had been wrong about the institution of that kingdom and about His future earthly reign, Jesus certainly would have been obligated to correct their misconception. After all, is He not the Truth? And as the Truth He cannot lie. If there was to be no future earthly reign of Jesus Christ, He should have said something like, "I am sorry, gentlemen, but you have it all wrong. You see, there really is no future for the nation of Israel. I really was only talking about a spiritual reign in men's hearts." But Jesus never said that! He simply said to His disciples that the question of the restoration of the kingdom was not their problem. He said, "It is not for you to know the times or dates the Father has set by his own authority" (Acts 1:7). He had a new plan, and they were going to be the ones to carry it out.

Jesus' command to His disciples was, "But you will receive power when the Holy Spirit comes on you; and you will be my witnesses in Jerusalem, and in all Judea and Samaria, and to the ends of the earth" (v. 8). The disciples were to begin where they were and, in ever-widening circles, take the message about Jesus Christ to the entire world. Ten days after Jesus spoke these words, Israel celebrated the Day of Pentecost (Acts 2).

Jesus had said that the disciples would be baptized with the Spirit "in a few days" in Acts 1:5. And since Acts 2 occurred just ten days later, the events that took place on the Day of Pentecost would seem to be the ones to which Jesus was pointing. But Acts 2 never specifically refers to the baptizing work of the Spirit. Many other spectacular manifestations of the Spirit are mentioned, such as a violent rushing wind, tongues of fire, and the ability of the disciples to speak in human languages they did not previously know (vv. 2–4). But the baptizing work of the Spirit is never mentioned. Is there any evidence that this new ministry of the Spirit began on that day? Yes, there is.

In Acts 10 Peter was sent by God to the household of a Gentile named Cornelius, who lived in the city of Caesarea. Peter had been prepared for this through a vision which God communicated to him in Joppa (vv. 9–16). The clear teaching of that vision was that there no longer was any distinction between what God considered "clean" and "unclean." While the vision focused on kosher and nonkosher animals, God was specifically referring to Jewish and Gentile people (vv. 28, 34–35). When

Peter came into Cornelius's house, he communicated to those present the truths about Jesus Christ (vv. 34–43), including His death and resurrection. When Cornelius heard the message, he and his household believed.

The Jewish brethren who had accompanied Peter were struck with amazement at this point because they saw the gift of the Holy Spirit poured out on the Gentiles. "For they heard them speaking in tongues and praising God" (Acts 10:46). As a result, Cornelius and his household were permitted to experience water baptism, so that there could be a public sign of their identification with Jesus Christ.

Peter realized that he had just experienced something new and significant. How would he explain what had happened to the Jewish brethren back in Jerusalem? The answer is seen in Acts 11, for it is clear that some took issue with what he had done (vv. 2–3). As Peter spoke to the brethren, he first told them of the vision God had given him (vv. 5–10). He then reported what happened when he began to preach, for those in Cornelius's household believed and "the Holy Spirit came on them as he had come on us at the beginning. Then I remembered what the Lord had said: 'John baptized with water, but you will be baptized with the Holy Spirit.' So if God gave them the same gift as he gave us, who believed in the Lord Jesus Christ, who was I to think that I could oppose God?" (vv. 15–17). Clearly, in the mind of Peter, Cornelius and his household had an experience similar to the disciples "at the beginning." And Peter also connected both events to the promised baptism of the Holy Spirit.

If the promise of the baptism of the Spirit is future in Acts 1, it has clearly taken place by the time we reach Acts 11. As one reads through each of those chapters, it certainly seems that the best and clearest place to put the first experience of the baptism of the Spirit is Acts 2.

But why is the baptizing work of the Holy Spirit so important? The answer to that question is seen when the primary intent of the baptizing work of the Spirit is declared by the apostle Paul. "For we were all baptized by one Spirit into one body—whether Jews or Greeks, slave or free—and we were all given the one Spirit to drink" (1 Cor. 12:13). It is the baptizing work of the Holy Spirit that places each individual who believes in Jesus Christ as his or her personal Savior into the body of Christ. And in Colossians 1:18 Paul states clearly that the body of Christ is the church. The church began when the baptizing work of the Holy Spirit began, because it is the Holy Spirit who baptizes believers into the body of Christ.

The church is something of far greater significance than the physical buildings that sit on street corners. It is not just an organized group of people who come together at various times throughout the week. In reality, the church is an invisible body of individuals who are joined to the risen Lord Jesus Christ through the baptizing work of the Holy Spirit. And since the baptizing work of the Holy Spirit began on the Day of Pentecost in Acts 2, that is also when the church began.

The church is a distinct entity from Israel. Israel was, and is, a nation made up of people from one ethnic group. Before the death of Christ, God worked through the nation of Israel to bring blessing to the world. Today God's primary work worldwide is the building of His church. As the followers of Jesus Christ continue to proclaim the glorious message of salvation through faith for all who will believe, the church, the invisible body of Christ, continues to grow. People from a multitude of ethnic, sociological, and economic backgrounds all share equally in the body of Christ. What a blessing it is to be part of the body of Jesus Christ today!

But the church has not replaced Israel . . . nor has she inherited the promises God made to Israel! In the present age, God has temporarily "set aside" Israel (Rom. 11:17–25). But the Bible clearly teaches that a time is coming when God will conclude His program for the church here on earth . . . and resume His program for the Jews. When will this take place?

DELIVERANCE VERSUS TRIBULATION

What does the Bible say is ahead for the world and for the church? As world events rush past, is there a plan of God that is being carried out? It does appear that there are at least two distinct periods of time still ahead for this world. Each must be examined separately.

The Coming Tribulation

The Scriptures speak of a coming time of trouble for the world often referred to as the Tribulation. Daniel refers to this period of time in his prophecy of "the seventy weeks" (9:24–27). A number of scholars have demonstrated that each of the "weeks" in Daniel's prophecy is a seven-year period of prophetic days (360-day years). The first sixty-nine weeks were fulfilled when Jesus Christ rode into the city of Jerusalem declaring Himself to be the King of the Jews on what is commonly called Palm Sunday. But what about the seventieth week of the prophecy? If each of the first sixty-nine weeks was a period of seven years directed toward the Jews and the city of Jerusalem, does that not imply that the seventieth week should also be a period of seven years with the same emphasis? Has the seventieth week found its fulfillment, or is it still a future period? Many believe that the coming Tribulation will be that final "week" of Daniel's prophecy. Through that seven-year period God will complete His plan for the nation of Israel.

The prophet Jeremiah refers to the period as a "time of trouble for Jacob" (30:7). Jeremiah pictures the period as a time of terrible persecution directed against Israel. "Cries of fear are heard—terror, not peace. Ask and see: Can a man bear children? Then why do I see every strong man with his hands on his stomach like a woman in labor, every face turned deathly pale? How awful that day will be! None will be like it. It will be a time of trouble for Jacob, but he will be saved out of it" vv. 5–7). By calling it a time of trouble *for Jacob*, the prophet seems to indicate that the focus of the period will be the nation Israel.

Jesus Christ spoke of this time in a message often called the Olivet Discourse (Matt. 24–25). The message grew out of a visit to the temple in Jerusalem. As Jesus and the disciples left the temple area, the disciples pointed out to Jesus the various temple buildings (24:1). Jesus replied that "not one stone here will be left on another; every one will be thrown down" (v. 2). The disciples then asked Jesus, "When will this happen, and what will be the sign of your coming and of the end of the age?" (v. 3). Their questions are clearly "Jewish," for they were concerned about what would happen to the city of Jerusalem and the temple, and what would be the sign of the Messiah's coming at the end of the age.

The Jews divided history into two ages: the present age (the "times of the Gentiles") and the age to come (the age of the Messiah and His kingdom). Jesus responded to these questions by explaining to His disciples the events that will lead up to His return to earth to inaugurate His Messianic Kingdom. He described the time immediately preceding His return as a time in which "there will be great distress, unequaled from the beginning of the world until now—and never to be equaled again" (Matt. 24:21). It is a time when "those who are in Judea" will need to "flee to the mountains" to escape (v. 16). Such a description from the Lord seems to characterize this coming period of tribulation as a time of intense persecution, a persecution for the nation Israel.

The Scriptures are consistent in their description of this future time of judgment coming on the earth. The prophets of the Old Testament and Jesus describe the time in a way that relates specifically to the nation Israel and the city of Jerusalem. But how does the church fit into this final seven-year period that precedes Christ's return to set up His kingdom? Is this a time of trouble that will be experienced by all believers . . . including the church? Are we destined to experience this time of wrath? The Bible says no!

The Promised Deliverance

The apostle Paul makes it clear that believers in Jesus Christ are not destined to experience the wrath of God. When writing to the church that existed in the city of Thessalonica, Paul spoke of how the believers there had "turned to God from idols to serve the living and true God, and to wait for his Son from heaven, whom he raised from the dead—Jesus, who rescues us from the coming wrath" (1 Thess. 1:9–10). Paul later wrote, "For God did not appoint us to suffer wrath but to receive salvation through our Lord Jesus Christ" (5:9). If the entire seventieth week of Daniel is characterized as a period of God's wrath, then how could believers who constitute the body of Jesus Christ today be included in that time? But did Jesus Christ give any indication as to the destiny of this church He said He would build?

On the last night that Jesus was alive in His physical body on earth, He met with His disciples in the Upper Room to observe the Passover. He knew He would be betrayed, illegally tried, and crucified. His offer of the promised Davidic kingdom had been rejected by the nation of Israel. Therefore the things He said to His disciples that evening were spoken to those who would soon be part of the church, the body of Christ. Jesus spoke to His disciples about the future. "Do not let your hearts be troubled. Trust in God; trust also in me. In my Father's house are many rooms; if it were not so, I would have told you. I am going there to prepare a place for you. And if I go and prepare a place for you, I will come back and take you to be with me that you also may be where I am" (John 14:1–3). Those words had never been heard before by the disciples. As Old Testament saints, their great hope was that Messiah would come to earth during their lifetime and institute His kingdom on the earth. But now Jesus was describing a different destiny . . . with a heavenly hope. He promised to return for His followers and to take them to His Father's house in heaven so that they could always be with Him there. This initial revelation of a new destiny for the church was later explained more fully by the apostle Paul.

Paul traveled throughout the Roman Empire and led many to Christ as Savior. He taught these new believers the truth that Jesus Christ could return at any moment. But as time passed, some of these new believers died. Paul wrote to the church in Thessalonica to remind them that they need not grieve like those without hope when confronted with the death of a believing loved one. All those believers who had died had gone to be with Jesus. And someday they would return with Him to be reunited with their physical bodies, which they left behind at death. Paul explained the specific order of events. "The dead in Christ will rise first. After that, we who are still alive and are left will be caught up together with them in the clouds to meet the Lord in the air. And so we will be with the Lord forever" (1 Thess. 4:16–17).

The event described by Paul is often referred to as the Rapture. This term comes from the Latin translation of the word for "caught up" in verse 17. While the word "rapture" does not appear in the Bible, the concept of a "catching up" is clearly taught in this passage.

Paul also wrote to the church in Corinth, to tell them about Christ's return . . . and our transformation. His focus in his letter to the Corinthians is not on what happens to dead believers as much as it is on what happens to living believers. Paul stated that he wanted to acquaint his readers with a "mystery" (1 Cor. 15:51). And what was the mystery that Paul wanted to reveal? "We will not all sleep, but we will all be changed." Paul was stating that there will be a generation of believers who will never experience physical death. When the Lord returns to rapture His church, all regenerated individuals will "in a flash" (v. 52) be changed. One second, believers will be moving around on this planet, but in the next second they will find themselves with Jesus Christ in God's house. What a glorious and blessed hope!

In the book of Revelation, the apostle John records seven letters from the Lord Jesus Christ to seven churches in Asia Minor. The Lord only has words of commendation for the church at Philadelphia (Rev. 3:7–13). To this faithful church the Lord promised, "Since you have kept my command to endure patiently, I will also keep you from the hour of trial that is going to come upon the whole world to test those who live on the earth" (v. 10). The period of judgment to which Jesus refers is the coming Tribulation, the seventieth week of Daniel's prophecy. The specific events that will happen during this period are recorded in Revelation 6–19. But Jesus promises that He will keep the church at Philadelphia from that hour. How will that be accomplished? The words of the Lord Jesus to this faithful church speak of removal from the very hour in which the trouble is to occur.

Suppose I were to say to some of my students at Moody Bible Institute, "Don't worry. Because you have been faithful, I will keep you from the hour in which the final exam for my course will occur." Does it sound like I would make them take the test . . . or even require them to sit through the test? Or would they assume I have exempted them from the period when everyone else must show up to take the test? So too the Lord promises His faithful believers that they will never enter into that period of judgment, the Tribulation, that is coming to test "earth dwellers." Believers, whose citizenship is in heaven above, look for a more blessed experience of removal from this earth to be joined with their Lord in heaven.

THE RAPTURE VERSUS THE SECOND COMING

It does appear from the Scriptures that there are two future events that must be kept distinct: the Rapture of the church and the second coming of Jesus Christ to earth to inaugurate the promised Davidic kingdom. There are some similarities between the two events, and that should not be a surprise because the Lord Jesus Christ is the focus of both. But the clear differences between the two events require us to keep them distinct.

When Jesus Christ returns at the time of the Rapture, "the dead in Christ" rise first (1 Thess. 4:16). Then "we who are still alive and are left will be caught up together with them in the clouds to meet the Lord in the air. And so we will be with the Lord forever" (v. 17). It does not appear that in the Rapture the Lord Jesus will return all the way to the earth, but living believers will meet Jesus Christ "in the air." This will be the fulfillment of Jesus' words in John 14:3 where He said that He would take believers to be with Him in His Father's house.

In contrast, when Jesus returns to earth at the Second Coming, His feet will touch the Mount of Olives. This will result in tremendous topographical changes. "The Mount of Olives will be split in two from east to west, forming a great valley, with half of the mountain moving north and half moving south" (Zech. 14:4). This return will fulfill the words spoken by the angels to the disciples on the Mount of Olives. "Men of Galilee . . . why do you stand here looking into the sky? This same Jesus, who has been taken from you into heaven, will come back in the same way you have seen him go into heaven" (Acts 1:11).

The Rapture of the church is the next prophetic event on God's calendar. There are no "signs" that must precede the Rapture, nor are there any prophecies that must be fulfilled. There is nothing standing in the way of Jesus' coming for His saints. Paul expected Christ's return for the church in his own lifetime. After talking about the effects of Christ's return in the air for "the dead in Christ," Paul then discussed the effects on those believers who will still be alive at that time: "After that, *we who are still alive and are left* will be caught up together with them in the clouds to meet the Lord in the air" (1 Thess. 4:17, italics added). Paul included himself with those anticipating Christ's return to take His church home to heaven at any time.

While there are no "signs of the times" that one must look for in anticipation of the Rapture, the Second Coming is a completely different matter. The seven-year period of Daniel 9 must be fulfilled, which includes the making—and breaking—of a covenant with Israel and the setting up of the "abomination that causes desolation" (v. 27). The gathering of the nations in battle against Jerusalem (Zech. 14) must take place. All the events of Revelation 6–19 must take place. The day and hour of Christ's physical return to earth might be a mystery, but Jesus told the disciples that these various signs would serve as signals that the end "is near, . . . right at the door" (Matt. 24:32–33).

CONCLUSION

I still chuckle a little when I remember my grandson's question, "Why do we always keep coming to church?" But it is clear that God's primary work today in the world revolves around His program for the church. The church began on the Day of Pentecost and will continue until the Rapture. Believers must always keep their eyes focused on the possibility that Jesus might come today. Truly that is our blessed hope!

THE NATIONS IN TRANSITION: THE SHAPE OF THE FINAL SUPERPOWER

✢

Dr. William H. Marty

> *Enough of blood and tears. Enough!*
> —YITZHAK RABIN

I have walked across the Temple Mount in Jerusalem on many occasions. But his walk was different. I walked there as a tourist to see the Dome of the Rock. His walk was intended to make a statement. I am not sure if he anticipated the resulting firestorm of violence. But in September 2000 when Ariel Sharon, the leader of Israel's right-wing opposition party, walked across the Temple Mount within sight of the Muslim shrine known as the Dome of the Rock, he ignited century-old fires of racial and religious hatred. The evening news pictured waves of Palestinians throwing rocks and firebombs at Israeli soldiers who responded with bullets and rockets. And an obvious casualty in the conflict was the most recent attempt to construct a lasting peace in the Middle East. But this is not the first time that the fires of hatred have consumed the hope for peace.

Why? Why haven't the nations, even the United States, been able to negotiate peace between Israel and its Arab neighbors? In order to answer this question, we need to put the dramatic collapse of the current attempt for peace in historical context.

"NEXT YEAR IN JERUSALEM"

Since A.D. 70, when the Romans captured Jerusalem and scattered the Jews among the nations, Jews have longed for a return to Zion, the land promised to Abraham, Isaac, and Jacob. This longing is expressed at the end of every Passover meal, a celebration that commemorates Israel's deliverance from Egyptian bondage, in the prayer, "next year in Jerusalem."

A defining moment for the return to the land came in 1877 when Naphtali Herz Imber, a Romanian Jew, penned a poem that eventually became the national anthem for the State of Israel. The words to *Hatikva* ("The Hope") read, in part:

> Our hope is not yet lost,
> The hope of two thousand years,
> To be free people in our land,
> The land of Zion and Jerusalem.

Deeply concerned by the anti-Semitic environment in Europe, Theodor Herzl became convinced that Jews needed a place of refuge. His endeavors culminated in 1896 when he published a book entitled *The Jewish State*. In it he boldly declared, "Palestine is our ever-memorable historic home." Though small, the book became the inspiration for the emergence of political

Zionism, and the first Zionist Congress was convened in Basel, Switzerland, on August 29, 1897. The Congress's strategy was twofold: "to strengthen Jewish consciousness and national feeling" and "to obtain the support of the various Governments of the world for the aims of Zionism."

The second defining moment for the establishment of a Jewish state came in 1917. A. J. Balfour, the British foreign secretary, declared Britain's support for a "Jewish National Home" in a letter to Lord Rothschild, a wealthy Jewish entrepreneur. He assured Rothschild that His Majesty's Government viewed "with favour the establishment in Palestine of a national home for the Jewish people. . . ." The Balfour Declaration stirred the hopes of Jews around the world for a homeland in Palestine and provided new momentum for immigration.

After World War I, the hope for a Jewish national homeland was in the hands of the League of Nations. At the Paris Peace Conference in 1917, after several from the Jewish delegation spoke passionately about the years of exile and suffering, the League granted the Palestine Mandate to Britain and acknowledged the intent of the Balfour Declaration. Though the British attempted to restrict immigration, thousands of Jews managed to return to Palestine. From 1922 to 1939 the Jewish population increased from 83,000 to 445,000.

But the greatest momentum for a Jewish state came from Hitler's horrific attempt to exterminate the Jewish people in the Holocaust. As survivors arrived in Palestine with shocking stories of what was happening in Europe, there was a renewed determination to form a Jewish state. The Jews of Palestine began organizing for a Jewish homeland and made preparations to fight, if necessary.

After World War II, the world could not ignore the death of approximately six million Jews at the hands of Nazi executioners, and in 1947 the General Assembly of the United Nations voted for the partition of Palestine. The United Nations thought it had done its duty. With the establishment of a Jewish state, the world believed that the Jewish people at last had their homeland where they could live in peace. But instead of providing a safe homeland for Jews, the end of the British Mandate marked the beginning of war. The new State of Israel found itself in a life-and-death struggle with invading Arab armies. Israel emerged as the victor in the 1948 "War of Independence" and found that it controlled more land than the United Nations had initially granted the new state.

Ironically, even the establishment of the State of Israel has not resulted in a safe and secure homeland for Jews but has instead fueled continuing fires of racial and religious hatred and violence. Since its first "War of Independence" in 1948, Israel has fought three major wars against antagonistic Arab states. In addition to the threat of war, Jews live daily with the danger of terrorist attacks and violent confrontations with Palestinians. Since 1987, Palestinians have engaged in an ongoing *intifada*, a term used to describe the militant uprising against Israel.

In 1989 the government of Israel launched a peace initiative that was later to become known as the "peace process." A major breakthrough occurred at the Madrid Conference in 1991. For the first time since the War of Independence, Israel and the Palestinians sat down at the negotiating table. The negotiations that were started at Madrid continued at Camp David in Washington, D.C., with Israel at least willing to discuss some kind of limited Palestinian authority. In spite of Israel's willingness to discuss Palestinian autonomy, the *intifada* continued. Autonomy was not enough; the Palestinians insisted on territorial sovereignty.

When Yitzhak Rabin became prime minister in 1992, he informed the Knesset that his government was willing to do everything possible to achieve peace and prevent war. He hoped that Israelis and Palestinians could become partners, not enemies, in the peace process. His agenda was revolutionary and designed to lead to a "permanent solution" to hostilities in the Middle East. Rabin concluded a speech to the Knesset with these words, "May the Lord give His people strength; may the Lord bless His people with peace." In spite of Rabin's willingness to pursue a new approach to peace, the terror continued inside Israel. Israeli security forces and Palestinians clashed daily.

At a secluded villa outside Oslo, Israel and the Palestinian Liberation Organization (PLO) began secret talks. After weeks of painful negotiations, the participants agreed on a Declaration of Principles that they hoped would normalize relations with the Palestinians. President Clinton invited Yitzhak Rabin and Yasser Arafat to Washington for a public signing of the document on the lawn of the White House. Millions watched on television as Rabin and Arafat shook hands to symbolize Israel's recognition of the Palestinian Liberation Organization. In his speech, Rabin spoke directly to Palestinians and closed with an emotional appeal, "We are today giving peace a chance and saying to you: Enough. Let's pray that a day will come when we all will say: Farewell to arms." But carrying out the Oslo Accord proved much more difficult than signing it. Extremists on both sides sought to sabotage it, and killings by both sides put intense pressure on the agreement.

Determined to make the Oslo Accord work, Shimon Peres went to Gaza for a meeting with Arafat. They agreed on a complex plan for the withdrawal of Israeli troops from designated areas and the transfer of control to the Palestinian Authority. The agreement, called Oslo II, was signed several weeks later on the White House lawn.

Though the hope for peace was only a slender thread, the "peace process" was still in place. At a mass rally in Tel Aviv, Rabin again made an emotional plea for peace to prevail over violence. "For them, for our children, in my case for our grandchildren, I want this government to exhaust every opening, every possibility, to promote and achieve a comprehensive peace. Even with Syria, it will be possible to make peace." The rally ended with the singing of "The Song of Peace." On the way to his car, Yitzhak Rabin was gunned down by a fanatical Jewish religious student.

President Clinton was among those who gave eulogies at Rabin's graveside. At the end of his speech, he whispered the words *Shalom haver,* "Peace, my friend." But the peace process was in serious jeopardy. Several suicide bombers struck in Jerusalem and Tel Aviv. The opposition party in Israel denounced the peace process as a total failure and insisted on "peace with security."

In October 1998, the United States made another attempt to end the hostilities between Israel and the Palestinian Authority. At the Wye River Conference Center in Maryland, the Palestinian Authority agreed to make a greater effort to stop terrorism and to remove from its charter a commitment to the destruction of Israel in exchange for additional territory. Once again, Israel hoped to exchange land for peace.

Unfortunately, a new millennium began with the nations still unable to resolve the ethnic and religious hatreds that have defied all attempts to achieve a lasting peace in the Middle East. The most recent crisis in Israel shows how easy it is for violence to spiral out of control. Ariel Sharon's walk across the Temple Mount in sight of the Dome of the Rock, a Muslim holy place, triggered a riot of rock-throwing Palestinians. This led to the televised death of a twelve-year-old boy who was accidentally shot as his father tried to shield him. The madness continued when two Israelis took a wrong turn and were arrested by the Palestinian police. While supposedly under police protection, they were seized and then murdered and mutilated by a blood-thirsty mob. Prime Minister Barak responded by ordering a helicopter attack on a compound near Arafat's headquarters. As violence swept across the West Bank and Gaza and spiraled out of control, Prime Minister Barak said that the window of peace may be closing.

IS PEACE POSSIBLE?

Was Prime Minister Barak right? Is the window of peace closing? Assuming that the peace process could somehow be restarted, is it realistic to think that the Israelis would ever trust the Palestinians as partners in peace? And would any concessions satisfy many Palestinians whose anger seemingly borders on an insane fanaticism and hatred of Israel?

No one would argue that the causes of the hostilities in the Middle East are many and incredibly complex. In fact, many say that they defy a solution. From a biblical perspective, however, the answer is as old as the first murder. Cain's lack of faith and reverence for God made his offering unacceptable, but Abel's offering pleased the Lord. Blinded by jealousy, Cain killed his brother. The problem was not political, racial, or religious. They were not divided by political ideologies, racial bigotry, or competing religious systems. Cain and Abel were brothers, born of the same parents. The problem was spiritual. God considered Abel's offering acceptable but was displeased by Cain's. And that's the problem in the Middle East today. Why did the peace process fail? It was an attempt to apply a political solution to a spiritual problem.

What about the future? Does the Bible give us any hint of what will happen in the Middle East? The answer is "yes," but what the Bible says about the future in the Middle East is frightening . . . yet true.

THE TIMES OF THE GENTILES

*"Jerusalem will be trampled on by the Gentiles
until the times of the Gentiles are fulfilled."*
—LUKE 21:24

In answer to His disciples' questions about the end of the age, Jesus' statement about "the times of the Gentiles" identifies a crucial period of history for understanding the current turmoil in Israel and helps answer the question why no one has been able to bring permanent peace to the Middle East.

The "times of the Gentiles" began when the Babylonians, led by Nebuchadnezzar, captured Jerusalem in 586 B.C. From the fall of Jerusalem in 586 B.C. to the present, Gentiles have either threatened or controlled Israel. Israel has experienced only two periods of independence. First, after approximately fifty years of brutal oppression by the Syrians (Seleucids) Israel fought and won their independence in 143 B.C. The nation, however, did not enjoy total security or genuine peace, but was under continuous threat from powerful nations and in constant turmoil because of internal power struggles. The Hasmonean State, as Israel was called, came to an abrupt end in 63 B.C. The Roman general Pompey captured Jerusalem, and Israel was eventually declared an imperial province of the Roman Empire. The second period of independence came in 1947. The United Nations General Assembly voted to partition Palestine and to establish Jewish and Arab states within the divided country. But even statehood did not bring peace; instead, hostilities in the Middle East intensified.

The Bible teaches that the "times of the Gentiles" will end with the second coming of Christ. This means that they will continue through the next period on God's prophetic calendar, the Tribulation. And then at the end of the seven-year Tribulation, Jesus Christ will return as Lord of lords and King of kings. He will crush all opposition, rescue the Jewish people, and establish a kingdom of righteousness and peace. Until the return of Christ, we should expect turmoil and trouble in Jerusalem and Israel. Because Jesus Christ predicted trouble for Jerusalem until His return, peace in the Middle East has eluded some of the world's greatest statesmen.

If we are in the "times of the Gentiles," this raises several questions about the future. Who will lead the final world government? What is the nature of the final Gentile world power? Is the United States mentioned in prophecy? What will happen when Christ returns to set up His kingdom?

The Bible does not answer these questions with the kind of specificity that we would like. Many have attempted to identify nations and individuals in the past and the present with the final world empire, only to end up with "egg on their face." The Bible does however paint in broad-brush strokes a fascinating picture of what will happen as we approach the end of the age. This picture is found primarily in two books of the Bible— Daniel and Revelation.

THE PEACEMAKER

A Man of Peace?

The Bible teaches that in "the last days" a charismatic individual will propel himself into prominence as a world leader by brokering peace with Israel. Who is this peacemaker and what is his political agenda? Though he is commonly referred to as the Antichrist, the Scriptures give him numerous other titles that are indicative of his character and his program.

He is identified as a "little horn" in Daniel 7:8. "While I was thinking about the horns, there before me was another horn, a little one." Daniel says that this little horn had "eyes like the eyes of a man and a mouth that spoke boastfully." The Antichrist is a man of strength. Horns on an animal represent its strength for attack and defense. He is intelligent ("the eyes of a man") and arrogant ("a mouth that spoke boastfully"). He defies God, persecutes the nation Israel, and brings Israel under his authority (v. 25).

He is simply called a "ruler" in Daniel 9:26, but what he accomplishes sets the stage for one of the most terrifying and destructive eras in the history of the world. According to verse 27, "the ruler" will make a covenant with Israel at the beginning of Daniel's Seventieth Week, or the future seven-year Tribulation period. As the head of a powerful coalition of nations, he guarantees the security of God's people. The treaty is a ruse, but it

will prove effective in convincing Israel that this ruler is the nation's best hope for peace. Unfortunately, in the middle of the
seven-year period, he will betray Israel and move to establish
himself as the political and religious ruler of the world. Though
he begins by promising peace, this ruler will ultimately set the
Middle East ablaze with destruction and death. His crowning
achievement will be his boldest and most despicable act. After
eradicating Israel's religious system, he will erect an image of
himself on the Temple Mount in Jerusalem, and compel the
world to worship him as God. Christ referred to this blasphe-
mous act when He warned His disciples about "'the abomination that causes desolation,' spoken of through the prophet
Daniel" (Matt. 24:15).

Paul calls this future leader "the man of lawlessness" and
"the man doomed to destruction" (2 Thess. 2:3). The title "man
of lawlessness" implies that the Antichrist is a ruthless, hard-
ened criminal who rejects all law, especially God's. But as Paul
indicates, he is also "the man doomed to destruction," a reference
to the fact that Christ will destroy him at His second coming
(v. 8). Paul gives perhaps the clearest reference to his blasphe-
mous attempt to make himself God in the middle of the Tribulation. Seeking to replace the worship of the one and only God, he
will proclaim that he is God and will set up a throne in the sanctuary of the temple (v. 4).

The current crisis in Israel gives us a preview of the betrayal
of the peace pact that the Antichrist will make with Israel at the
beginning of the Tribulation. In the words of one reporter, the
mutual agreement that Israel hoped would lead to permanent
peace was killed—"not by some unknown crazed fanatic, but by
a Nobel Peace Prize winner and one of its godfathers" (*U.S.*

News & World Report, November 6, 2000, p. 92). Yasser Arafat, the leader of the Palestinian Authority and ironically a Nobel Peace Prize recipient, shook hands on the lawn of the White House and ostensibly agreed to become a partner in peace with Yitzhak Rabin. But either by design or default, he has become the leader of one the most vicious and potentially dangerous confrontations in recent history. The mob warfare in the West Bank has the potential to escalate beyond an ethnic struggle between Israelis and Palestinians to a war between Jews and Muslims. The recent violence even has its own "mini abomination of desolation." When the Israelis relinquished control of Joseph's tomb, a Jewish holy site, to the Palestinians, fanatical Muslims torched it, hastily built a new structure, and painted it Islamic green.

John calls the Antichrist "a beast coming out of the sea" in Revelation 13:1. The sea symbolizes the demonic origin of the Antichrist. According to Revelation 11:7, he came out of the "Abyss" (cf. 17:8), the source of satanic opposition to God. The Antichrist is a henchman of Satan and the second person in an unholy trinity made up of the Dragon (Satan) and "another beast, coming out of the earth" (13:11). Satan's goal from the beginning has been to overthrow God and to rule the world. At the end of the age, he will turn to two beasts, forming an unholy trinity that is a clever and sinister imitation of God the Father, God the Son, and God the Holy Spirit. Satan assumes the place of God, the Antichrist the place of Christ, and the False Prophet the place of the Holy Spirit.

John adds that "the beast" has seven heads and ten horns with ten crowns on his ten horns (Rev. 13:1). The ten horns connect the Antichrist with the fourth beast in Daniel 7, which also had ten horns. According to Revelation 17:12, the ten horns are ten kings, who will become allies with the Antichrist to form an empire that is incredibly powerful and as evil as it is powerful. John's description becomes even more chilling when he reveals that the Antichrist is energized by Satan (13:2). He gains world renown when he makes an amazing recovery from what is apparently a mortal wound (v. 3). Since only God has the ultimate power over life and death, it is unlikely that the Antichrist is resurrected from the dead. He is either supernaturally healed or at least gives the appearance that he has recovered from a fatal wound.

In either case, the deception works; "the whole world was astonished and followed the beast" (Rev. 13:3). The world not only worships the Beast, but they also worship Satan. Satan has thus achieved his ultimate goal, to usurp God and to receive worship that God alone deserves. Satan assumes the place of God, and the Beast or the Antichrist pretends that he is a new messiah. Once he has consolidated his power, achieving total political and spiritual domination over the entire world, the Antichrist goes on a rampage of terror against the Tribulation saints.

Though he controls Israel, even that does not satisfy the Antichrist's thirst for power and honor. Daniel 11 says that midway through the Tribulation he will use his political and military might to claim absolute power in the religious realm. Like the infamous Antiochus Epiphanes, who ruthlessly persecuted Jews in the second century B.C., the Antichrist will blaspheme God, disregard all organized religion, repudiate all messianic hopes, and magnify himself as God (vv. 37–38).

The Antichrist is not the only beast that will threaten the world in the Tribulation. In addition to the "beast coming out of the sea," John sees a beast "coming out of the earth" (Rev. 13:11). The second beast, or the "False Prophet" as he is commonly called, will work in close association with the Antichrist. Just as the Antichrist serves on behalf of Satan, the "false prophet" promotes the worship of the Antichrist. His activities are somewhat similar to the prophet Elijah's ministry. Like Elijah, he will perform spectacular signs and wonders. He is extremely persuasive and deceives many to worship the first beast. One of his intriguing and perplexing feats is somehow infusing life into an image of the Antichrist, even making it speak. And he will order the death of all those who refuse to worship the image.

This second leader will also control the world's economic system. Without a mark of 666 on either their right hand or forehead to prove that they worship the beast, no one will be allowed to buy or sell (Rev. 13:16–17). Though many have attempted to use the number 666 to identify a specific individual, the most we can say is that six is one less than the perfect number seven, the number for deity. The threefold repetition of the number suggests that Satan, the Antichrist, and the False Prophet are not divine. The unholy trinity is a clever and sinister counterfeit of God the Father, God the Son, and God the Holy Spirit but a pathetic failure in its attempt to replace the true Trinity of 777.

The Antichrist and the False Prophet are powerful, but they are no match for Christ. When Jesus Christ returns as King of kings and Lord of lords, He will cast both the Antichrist and the False Prophet into the lake of fire.

The Prince of Peace

"O Jerusalem, Jerusalem, you who kill the prophets and stone those sent to you, how often I have longed to gather your children together, as a hen gathers her chicks under her wings, but you were not willing. Look, your house is left to you desolate. For I tell you, you will not see me again until you say, 'Blessed is he who comes in the name of the Lord'" (Matt. 23:37–39).

In His final lament for the city of Jerusalem, Jesus warned that God would temporarily abandon His people for rejecting His Son. But God keeps His promises—always. His promises to Abraham and his descendants are unconditional, so God is not finished with Israel. Jesus will come to Israel a second time, and at His second coming Israel will accept, not reject, Him as their Lord and King.

One of God's primary purposes for the future Tribulation period is to break the stubborn hearts of His covenant people. The horrors of the Tribulation plus the testimony of a host of faithful witnesses will spark a spiritual awakening in Israel. Many will turn to Christ during the Tribulation, and many will die for their faith. When Jesus finally returns in power and glory, the nation Israel will experience the deep anguish of someone who realizes that he has made a terrible mistake. Instead of mocking and condemning Jesus as they did at His first coming, they will mourn and weep because they will recognize that Jesus was indeed Israel's true Messiah and King and that He is coming to judge them for rejecting Him. But their mourning will turn to rejoicing when they realize that the Lord has not come to punish but to rescue His people.

The Antichrist will consolidate his armies in the Middle East to crush the rebellion in Israel that was provoked by his breaking of the treaty with Israel and his desecration of the temple with his image. Some of the combatants will have been lured to the battle by demons (Rev. 16:12–16). When the total annihilation of God's covenant people seems inevitable, Jesus Christ suddenly appears riding on a white horse leading the armies of heaven. He treads on the armies of earth as one treads grapes in a winepress. Nothing in the history of war compares to the carnage of this final battle. With apocalyptic imagery, John sees an angel calling for the birds of heaven to gorge themselves at "the great supper of God" (Rev. 19:17–18). With the defeat of the godless forces of the Antichrist, the nation Israel will at last enjoy rest in the Promised Land and peace in Jerusalem.

The defeat of the Antichrist also sets the stage for the millennial (thousand-year) reign of Christ. Christ will establish Himself as King. He will cast the Antichrist and the False Prophet into the lake of fire, and He will bind Satan for a thousand years. He will rule the earth in peace and righteousness and fulfill the covenants that He made with Abraham and his descendants.

WHERE DOES AMERICA FIT IN PROPHECY?

"Is America mentioned in prophecy?" is one of the first questions that pops into a person's mind whenever the topic of discussion is prophecy. To find the United States in the Bible, you must use a highly imaginative interpretative process. Some think passages such as Isaiah 18, Jeremiah 50–51, and Revelation 18 contain figurative references to the United States, but it is a huge interpretive stretch to identify references to Cush and Babylon as the United States. After more than twenty years of studying and teaching the Bible, I am convinced that God's Word does not mention, directly or even symbolically, the United States.

This is not surprising for two reasons. First, the primary interest of the prophets was those nations in the Middle East that had a direct influence on Israel. Thus, you will find numerous references to ancient superpowers such as Egypt, Assyria, Babylon, and Persia. The Old Testament also contains references to smaller nations that were immediately adjacent to Israel, such as Edom, Moab, Ammon, Aram, Phoenicia, and Philistia. Second, as the end times unfold God will have the world's focus again turn to Israel and the Middle East. The United States may be the most important nation today, but God has a way of setting up nations—and tearing down nations—to further His prophetic plans.

CONCLUSION—
SHOULD WE ATTEMPT PEACE TODAY?

Pray for the peace of Jerusalem.
—PSALM 122:6

Will there be peace in Israel? Yes, someday, and perhaps even soon! But it will not be peace on a piece of paper. It will a real peace—a *shalom*. *Shalom* is a Hebrew word that means more than a cessation of hostilities. It is a positive word, indicating a sense of security based on a right relationship with God. *Shalom* includes completeness, health, justice, prosperity, and protection. When will this happen? When the Prince of Peace, the Lord Jesus Christ, comes a second time. He will rule with justice and righteousness. He will bring peace to Israel and to the world because He Himself is peace.

Since the Bible teaches that lasting peace will not come to Israel and the Middle East until the Prince of Peace returns, it may seem useless to some to work for peace in the Middle East. I don't think that is the right attitude for two reasons. First, we do not know God's timetable for the end of the age. Some believe that the current crises in the Middle East signal that we are in the last days. They may be right, but they may also be mistaken. Doomsday prophets have predicted the end of the world in the past, and nothing happened. People who set dates either do not know or have forgotten that Jesus said that angels and even the Son do not know the "day or hour" of His coming. Only God the Father knows the exact time of the end (Matt. 24:36). That means that current events in Israel may not be the beginning of the end. If not, then the United States and other nations should do everything within their power to reduce the tensions and resolve the grievances in the Middle East. Just as our nation promotes peace in other places in the world, it should attempt to bring peace to Israel. It is the right and humane thing to do!

Second, the psalmist exhorts us to pray for the peace of Jerusalem (Ps. 122:6), and Jesus exhorted believers to "be at peace with each other" (Mark 9:50). God wants people to live in harmony and peace. As believers we should pray for justice and peace to prevail over injustice and hatred in the Middle East.

The ultimate solution to the hostilities in the Middle East is spiritual not political. Real peace can only come when people are right with God, who is the source of peace. To live in peace with one another, both Arabs and Jews need to know God. When people are at peace with the God of peace, then they will be at peace with one another.

Jesus told His disciples, "Salt is good, but if it loses it saltiness, how can you make it salty again? Have salt in yourselves, and be at peace with each other" (Mark 9:50). Just as salt adds flavor to the food we eat, so also we should "flavor" the world in which we live. We *salt* the world when we live in peace and harmony with others and spread the message of God's love—a love that was incarnated in His Son, Jesus Christ, the Prince of Peace!

JERUSALEM:
THE EYE OF THE STORM
✳

Dr. Charles H. Dyer

> *This is what the Sovereign LORD says:*
> *This is Jerusalem, which I have set in the center of*
> *the nations, with countries all around her.*
> —EZEKIEL 5:5
>
> *Without Jerusalem, we are a body without a soul.*
> —DAVID BEN-GURION

THE CENTRALITY OF JERUSALEM

The world watched as President Clinton tried to "grab for the brass ring" to secure a foreign policy legacy for his presidency. The prize? A comprehensive peace between Israel and the Palestinians brokered by the White House. Meetings at Wye River and Camp David brought the elusive treaty almost within the President's reach . . . only to have the entire process self-destruct in a hail of rocks, Molotav cocktails, and rubber-coated bullets. What happened?

President Clinton, along with most of the Western news media, misunderstood the fundamental problem in the Middle East. They assumed the conflict between Israel and the Palestinians had social, economic, or political roots. That is, they believed the fundamental problem could be traced back to Palestinian nationalism or poverty or the plight of refugees. Western leaders, including Clinton, assumed that if they could fashion a Palestinian state, provide economic aid to "jump start" a shattered economy, and solve the refugee problem, they could bring peace to the Middle East. But they ignored the most basic issue behind the current Middle East crisis . . . religion. The struggle between Israel and the Palestinians is, in reality, a struggle to determine whose God is supreme. And Jerusalem is the central battleground.

Jerusalem's Importance to Jews

Jerusalem is the spiritual heart of Judaism. God summoned Abraham to offer Isaac as a sacrifice on Mount Moriah (Gen. 22:2). A thousand years later Solomon built his temple to the Lord on the same mountain (2 Chron. 3:1). Solomon's father, King David, chose Jerusalem to be the capital for the nation of Israel (2 Sam. 5:6–10). And David purchased the land on Mount Moriah where the temple would eventually stand (1 Chron. 21:18–22:1). Jerusalem was the place God chose "from among all your tribes to put his Name there for his dwelling" (Deut. 12:5).

Later, when Nebuchadnezzar destroyed Jerusalem and took the Jews into captivity in Babylon, the city was still foremost in their minds and hearts. "By the rivers of Babylon we sat and wept when we remembered Zion. . . . If I forget you, O Jerusalem, may my right hand forget its skill. May my tongue cling to the roof of my mouth if I do not remember you, if I do not consider Jerusalem my highest joy" (Ps. 137: 1, 5–6).

The Jewish people returned from Babylon to reclaim the land and rebuild their city. A new temple, though modest in comparison to the one built by Solomon, again graced Mount Moriah. It took an additional eighty years for Jerusalem's walls to be rebuilt, but God raised up Nehemiah to complete the task. Nehemiah records the adversity and opposition his people faced during these times of turmoil and triumph.

From the close of the Old Testament to the beginning of the New Testament, the Jewish people occupied the land and worshiped at their temple. But there was one notable exception. In 169 B.C., Antiochus IV Epiphanes plundered the temple, converting it into a pagan shrine to Zeus. He actively persecuted anyone who dared to resist or who sought to follow the Law of Moses. God raised up an elderly priest, Mattathias, and his son, Judas Maccabeus ("Judah the Hammer") to drive the Syrians from Jerusalem and to rededicate the temple to the Lord. This victory is recounted in the Jewish Feast of Hanukkah.

By the time of Jesus, Herod the Great had renovated and enlarged the temple. It was once again a place of beauty. The platform built by Herod to hold the expanded temple is, today, the same platform on which the Al Aksa mosque and the Dome of the Rock sit. This was the temple admired by the disciples (Matt. 24–25). But, as Jesus predicted in the Olivet Discourse, Jerusalem and the temple were again destroyed.

In A.D. 70 the Roman army attacked Jerusalem in response to the Jewish revolt that began four years earlier. Rome killed thousands of Jews and deported thousands more to be sold as slaves. A new Diaspora began that lasted for nineteen centuries. But during all those years the focus for the Jewish people was Jerusalem and their temple. As the Jewish Midrash so eloquently exclaimed, "The land of Israel is at the center of the world; Jerusalem is at the center of the land of Israel; the temple is at the center of Jerusalem."

Even into the twentieth century the soul of Judaism remained bound to Jerusalem. Rabbi Avraham Yitzchak HaCohen Kook wrote in 1921, "The voice which accompanies us with its pleasant hope twice a year, on the first night of Pesach and in the concluding prayer of Yom Kippur, is the voice of the soul of the Nation expressing its deepest desire: 'Next Year in Jerusalem.'" The horrors of the Holocaust only confirmed the necessity for providing the Jews with a homeland where they could find protection and fulfill their heartfelt desire once again to be a nation. Where should they go? Israel! What city should be their capital? Jerusalem!

But why does Israel's return to the land so inflame the Palestinians?

Jerusalem's Importance to Muslims

Islam teaches that Allah is the supreme God and that Jesus Christ is not the divine Son of God. He was merely a prophet, like Moses, in a long line of messengers that culminated in the final prophet, Muhammad. According to Islamic teaching, Judaism was supplanted by Christianity, and Christianity has been supplanted by Islam. Muslims confidently assert that their religion is destined to triumph over its earlier, imperfect predecessors; and they believe God has commanded them to spread the truth of Islam around the world.

Land conquered for Allah remains the possession of Allah. No one has the right to give it away. That's why the Arab nations responded so viscerally to the establishment of the State of

Israel. Land that belonged to Allah since the earliest Muslim conquests—land they had fought to reclaim at the time of the Crusades—was to be given to a people who had been rejected by Allah because of their disobedience. Thus the very existence of Israel was an affront to Islam. But if the establishment of the nation Israel is an agitation, having the capital of that nation in Jerusalem is abhorrent . . . and having the Jews control the third holiest shrine of Islam is an utter abomination.

Jerusalem did not play a central role in the establishment of Islam. The two holiest cities are Mecca and Medina in Saudi Arabia because these are the cities where Muhammad began preaching and where he fled into exile when his message was initially rejected. However, Muslim tradition does hold Jerusalem in high regard. It teaches that the Temple Mount—the spot where the first temple from the time of Solomon and the second temple from the time of Jesus once stood—is the place from which Muhammad ascended to heaven on his night journey. Because of this, Jerusalem—and especially *Haram esh-Sharif,* the "noble sanctuary"—is viewed as the third holiest spot in Islam. The Arabic name for Jerusalem is *Al-Quds*—the holy place.

Two groups of people both claim the same city . . . and both have deep religious attachment to the same holy hill in that city. President Clinton's peace initiative failed because, like those who tried before, he couldn't find a way to satisfy the conflicting religious claims of both groups.

WHO OWNS THE CITY?

Up until the present time, every agreement reached between Israel and her Arab neighbors put off the issue of Jerusalem's sovereignty until a later date. The original Camp David Accords

—signed in 1978 by President Carter, Anwar al-Sadat of Egypt, and Menachem Begin of Israel—only came to pass after the participants agreed to defer discussions on Jerusalem. The 1993 Olso Accord placed the discussion of Jerusalem at the end of the process. Those involved in the negotiations realized the difficulty surrounding Jerusalem. They hoped that, by postponing all discussions on Jerusalem until the end, the momentum for peace would allow the negotiators to achieve a breakthrough. How wrong they were!

With peace seeming to be almost within their grasp, the negotiators tried to tackle the issue of sovereignty for Jerusalem. To whom does the city, including the Temple Mount, really belong? Semantic compromises were floated like trial balloons, only to be shot down by one side or the other. Shared sovereignty. Divine sovereignty with the present status quo. U.N. Security Council supervision over the Temple Mount with Muslim custodianship. No proposal was acceptable to all parties.

The game of diplomatic charades that extended through the Clinton presidency came to an abrupt end in September 2000 when Ariel Sharon, the leader of Israel's Likud party, took a walk on the Temple Mount. The talks broke down immediately, and the stones and bullets began to fly. Why did this one stroll cause so much turmoil?

Everyone recognized that the negotiators were trying to bring about an agreement by resorting to trickery, double-talk, and obfuscation. Both sides hoped to use the diplomatic loopholes to their ultimate advantage. But Ariel Sharon's walk on the Temple Mount highlighted the one central issue the negotiators were trying to ignore. His presence on the disputed site said, in effect, "You Palestinians think you will have control over this area, but that will never happen. We have a right to be here, and I'm telling you that we have no intention of giving up that right." His message came through, loud and clear, and so did the answer from the Palestinians.

What is the future for Jerusalem and the Middle East? Will peace talks ever succeed? President Clinton tried to revive the talks, and so will President Bush. A temporary calm may indeed return to the Middle East, but it will not be the comprehensive peace sought by so many for so long. The sticking point for any lasting agreement will be the status of Jerusalem and the Temple Mount.

JERUSALEM'S ROLE IN THE FUTURE

God has placed Jerusalem in the eye of the storm. As we approach the days leading up to the second coming of Jesus Christ, Jerusalem and the Temple Mount will be at the center of the conflict. The Bible describes five future scenes that are all set in Jerusalem. Taken together they enable us to understand what lies ahead for Jerusalem.

Jerusalem Will Dominate the World's Attention

The prophet Zechariah lived at the time of the nation's return to the land following their seventy-year captivity in Babylon. Zechariah encouraged the people to rebuild the temple, but he also prophesied of events that were far distant from his day. In chapters 9–14 the prophet had two extended prophecies (called "oracles" or "burdens") that provide a detailed account of the first and second comings of Israel's Messiah. The events of the first coming, which centered in Jerusalem, were dramatically fulfilled.

Zechariah 9:9   The Messiah rode into Jerusalem on a "colt, the foal of a donkey."

Zechariah 11:12–13   The Messiah was sold for thirty pieces of silver, which were then thrown "into the house of the LORD to the potter."

Zechariah's second message (chaps. 12–14) focuses on events leading up to the second coming of the Messiah. And ground zero for these events is Jerusalem! "I am going to make Jerusalem a cup that sends all the surrounding peoples reeling. Judah will be besieged as well as Jerusalem. On that day, when all the nations of the earth are gathered against her, I will make Jerusalem an immovable rock for all the nations. All who try to move it will injure themselves" (Zech. 12:2–3).

The last days will be a time when Israel and Jerusalem dominate the world's attention, though in a negative way. Nations will try to "move" God's people, but none will succeed. While this refers in a general way to "all the nations of the earth," Zechariah also underscores Israel's ongoing conflict with her surrounding neighbors. These will be the countries with whom Israel will experience the greatest conflict, and who will suffer defeat at Israel's hands. "They [i.e., Israel] will consume right and left all the surrounding peoples, but Jerusalem will remain intact in her place" (Zech. 12:6).

As the end times draw near, watch the tension increase between Israel and the surrounding Arab nations. Much of this conflict will center on their desire to wrest control of Jerusalem from Israel.

A Peace Treaty Will Be Signed

The world stands by and holds its collective breath whenever Israel and her neighbors are at war, because it fears two things. First, it fears that the Arab world will retaliate against the West by withholding oil and creating another economic crisis in the industrialized countries that are so dependent on oil from the Middle East. Second, it is afraid that Israel will feel threatened enough to unleash its nuclear arsenal . . . and draw the rest of the world into a nuclear war.

As a result, the United States, the European community, and a number of individual countries have proposed plans to bring peace to the Middle East. And, thus far, they have all failed. But Daniel 9:27 says the final seven-year period leading up to the second coming of Christ will begin when a coming ruler "will confirm a covenant with many for one 'seven.'" Daniel identifies this ruler by associating him with the nation that destroyed Jerusalem in A.D. 70. Rome destroyed Jerusalem, so this future ruler must be the leader of a revived Roman Empire.

Daniel states two key points about the treaty to be confirmed. First it will be made with "many." This could refer to a plurality within Israel (i.e., many of the Jewish people), or it could refer to a plurality of the people who are the subject of the covenant (i.e., Israel and the surrounding nations). It might be a treaty between this individual granting Israel his protection, or, perhaps more likely, it is a treaty between Israel and the surrounding nations brokered and guaranteed by this individual.

Second, the agreement will be designed to last for a "week" of years. That is, it will be a treaty with a seven-year time frame. We are not told why it is seven years in length, but it seems to be designed to give Israel genuine peace. Only in the middle of the period will the true intent of this ruler become evident . . . and Israel's peace be shattered.

Could this "covenant" be some type of Middle East peace treaty that has eluded world leaders for so long? It seems that this is likely because the end times begin with a great promise of peace. Paul wrote about the coming day of the Lord, and he said it would begin at a time when the world thinks peace is at hand. "While people are saying, 'Peace and safety,' destruction will come on them suddenly, as labor pains on a pregnant woman, and they will not escape" (1 Thess. 5:3).

The world yearns for peace in the Middle East, and it will someday come. But that peace will only be a transitory illusion. It will be engineered by one who initially rides onto the world scene on a "white horse," appearing to an unsuspecting world like another Jesus Christ (Rev. 6:2). But instead of his ushering in lasting peace, forces will be unleashed "to take peace from the earth and to make men slay each other" (v. 4).

Israel Will Be Allowed to Rebuild Her Temple

In the Jewish Quarter of the Old City of Jerusalem stands a small museum housing utensils, clothing, and musical instruments. The display is unremarkable until one realizes its significance comes from its connection to the future, not the past. The museum is called the Treasures of the Temple museum, and the items on display are being built for use in a new Jewish temple. The group is known as the Temple Mount Faithful, and they are committed to rebuilding a new temple . . . in Jerusalem . . . on the Temple Mount.

This group, though still a minority even among the religious Jews, believes that the only way they can truly worship

God in the land is through the temple sacrifices and services. While most orthodox Jews are waiting for the Messiah to come before rebuilding the temple, this group believes they must build the temple before the Messiah will return.

The Bible consistently pictures a temple in operation during the last days leading up to the second coming of Christ. Daniel 9:27 says that in the middle of the seven-year treaty the future leader will break his agreement and "put an end to sacrifice and offering. And on a wing of the temple he will set up an abomination that causes desolation." For this to be fulfilled, there needs to be a temple and the resumption of animal sacrifices. Jesus also predicted that there would be a temple in the end times. He told His disciples, "So when you see standing in the holy place 'the abomination that causes desolation' spoken of through the prophet Daniel—let the reader understand—then let those who are in Judea flee to the mountains" (Matt. 24:15–16).

Some years later, the apostle Paul reminded the church at Thessalonica that one of the key events in the future was the appearance in the temple of this future leader of evil. "He [i.e., this future Antichrist] will oppose and will exalt himself over everything that is called God or is worshiped, so that he sets himself up in God's temple, proclaiming himself to be God" (2 Thess. 2:4).

But in the present political climate how could the Jews ever build their temple? Wouldn't that cause a "holy war" that would bring millions of frenzied Muslims marching against Jerusalem? Perhaps. But it's also possible that events leading up to the seven-year treaty will allow this future world leader to extract concessions from the Arab nations that no one else has been able to achieve. In any case, the Bible says a temple will be built. But where will it be put?

Both Solomon's temple and Herod's temple stood on the site now occupied by the Dome of the Rock. This seems to be a settled fact of archaeology, but it's not universally accepted within Judaism. Several groups have proposed alternate locations on the Temple Mount. One individual, Asher Kaufmann, believes the temple and inner court stood to the north of the present-day Dome of the Rock. He has drawn plans that show how a temple and inner courtyard could be constructed without destroying the Muslim structure.

Does the Bible help in identifying where the temple will stand? The one passage that offers such a glimpse is Revelation 11:1–2. The apostle John was told to measure "the temple of God and the altar" but to "exclude the outer court." Why was he not to measure the outer court? "Because it has been given to the Gentiles." This future temple will, evidently, not have an outer court in the same way that Herod's temple did. Instead, that space will be given to non-Jews.

The Jews will likely build their future temple on the Temple Mount. If they decide the temple should stand to the north of the Dome of the Rock, then they could build the temple and inner court while allowing both the Dome and the Al Aksa mosque to remain. But if they build their temple where earlier structures stood, then the Dome of the Rock would need to be removed. However, the Al Aksa mosque could still remain if the outer court is, indeed, "given to the Gentiles."

Will there be a temple? Yes. Will it be as extensive as previous ones? Likely not, since the outer court belongs to the Gentiles. But a temple, and sacrifices, do play a role in Israel's future.

Jerusalem Will Be "Ground Zero" for the Activities of the Antichrist

Jerusalem is not the largest city in the world, nor is it the most geographically significant. But the Bible predicts that it will become "ground zero" for the future activities of the Antichrist. As the prophet Daniel described in advance the final campaign of the Antichrist, he wrote that, at the "time of the end," this future world dictator will be involved in fierce fighting and will "invade the Beautiful Land" (Dan. 11:40–41). After a series of campaigns, the Antichrist will reach his final objective . . . Jerusalem. "He will pitch his royal tents between the seas [i.e., the Mediterranean Sea and Dead Sea] at the beautiful holy mountain" (v. 45). Zechariah the prophet also identified Jerusalem as the location for the final battle of the ages. "I will gather all the nations to Jerusalem to fight against it" (Zech. 14:2).

Why will Jerusalem become ground zero? The reason is theological, not geographical. God chose Abraham and his descendants through Isaac to be the people through whom His blessings would flow out to all the earth. The Jews have been, are, and will remain God's Chosen People. The land of Israel is the real estate God promised to the Jews as their homeland. And Jerusalem is the city selected by God to be the place where His glory would visibly dwell among His people . . . and where His Ruler would rule over His people. The land of Israel . . . and the city of Jerusalem . . . and the Jews represent God's plan, God's promise, God's people, and God's power.

Satan has opposed God's plan from the beginning. He was in the Garden of Eden, he incited Herod to kill the babies of Bethlehem, and he entered into Judas's heart to betray the Lord. Satan's attacks will intensify as he seeks to thwart God's plans for the second coming of Christ. If he could not destroy Christ at His first coming, then he will try to destroy the nation of Israel prior to Christ's second coming.

In Revelation 12 God summarizes Satan's activity at Christ's first coming and during the time prior to His second coming. Before Christ returns again to claim His kingdom, Satan will be cast out of heaven, and he will work with all his demonic fury "because he knows that his time is short" (v. 12). Who will be the primary object of his attacks? He will pursue "the woman [Israel] who had given birth to the male child [Jesus]" and "the rest of her offspring [the Jews]" (vv. 13, 17). Israel and Jerusalem will be "ground zero" because they will be the special objects of Satan's fury.

Jesus Christ Will Return to this Earth at Jerusalem

If Jerusalem is "ground zero" for Satan's final assault, then it will also be "ground zero" for God's gracious redemption. Having announced the final attack against Jerusalem, the prophet Zechariah also announced that Jerusalem would be the location of the Messiah's glorious return to earth. "Then the LORD will go out and fight against those nations, as he fights in the day of battle. On that day his feet will stand on the Mount of Olives, east of Jerusalem, and the Mount of Olives will be split in two from east to west, forming a great valley, with half of the mountain moving north and half moving south. . . . Then the LORD my God will come, and all the holy ones with him" (Zech. 14:3–5).

On the day Jesus ascended to heaven He took His disciples "to the vicinity of Bethany" (Luke 24:50) on the Mount of Olives. As the disciples watched, "he was taken up before their very eyes, and a cloud hid him from their sight" (Acts 1:9).

Then two heavenly messengers announced to the disciples, "This same Jesus, who has been taken from you into heaven, will come back in the same way you have seen him go into heaven" (v. 11).

The Mount of Olives guards the eastern approach to Jerusalem. It witnessed Christ's triumphal entry into Jerusalem. It witnessed His ascension into heaven. And, someday, it will witness His glorious return.

WILL JERUSALEM
EVER EXPERIENCE PEACE?

The Mount of Olives is one of my favorite places in all Jerusalem. Standing there, gazing down on the Dome of the Rock, reminds me of the time when Jesus wept over Jerusalem (Luke 19:41–44) and, later, announced that the city would be "trampled on by the Gentiles until the times of the Gentiles are fulfilled" (21:24). That gold-gilded Dome, and the hatred spewed out against Israel from the mosques nearby, are tangible reminders that Christ's announcement of trouble for Israel during the times of the Gentiles is still taking place.

But then I turn and look back up the mountain and realize that, someday, He will return from heaven to again walk on this earth. And this is the spot where He will descend! This mountain —that now seems so permanent—will split apart at His coming. And the city that has seen so much strife, hatred, and bloodshed will finally experience peace. "It will be inhabited; never again will it be destroyed. Jerusalem will be secure" (Zech. 14:11).

When will peace come to Jerusalem? The world will think it has arrived when a future world leader makes a seven-year treaty that promises security for Israel and permits the rebuild-

ing of the temple. But this peace will be illusionary and fleeting
. . . a satanic counterfeit designed to deceive and seduce. It will
be the prelude to a time of terrible trouble for Israel and Jerusalem that will only end when the Messiah returns to this earth.

True peace will only come to Jerusalem when the Prince of
Peace returns to this earth to claim His throne.

> "For to us a child is born, to us a son is given, and the gov-
> ernment will be on his shoulders. And he will be called Wonder-
> ful Counselor, Mighty God, Everlasting Father, Prince of Peace.
> Of the increase of his government and peace there will be no end.
> He will reign on David's throne and over his kingdom, establish-
> ing and upholding it with justice and righteousness from that
> time on and forever. The zeal of the LORD Almighty will accom-
> plish this" (Isa. 9:6–7).

> "'But you, Bethlehem Ephrathah, though you are small
> among the clans of Judah, out of you will come for me one who
> will be ruler over Israel, whose origins are from of old, from an-
> cient times.' Therefore Israel will be abandoned until the time
> when she who is in labor gives birth and the rest of his brothers
> return to join the Israelites. He will stand and shepherd his flock
> in the strength of the LORD, in the majesty of the name of the
> LORD his God. And they will live securely, for then his greatness
> will reach to the ends of the earth. And he will be their peace"
> (Mic. 5:2–5).

Jerusalem, the city of peace, will only know true peace
when the Prince of Peace returns to rule the nations from her
midst. Until then, the city will remain in the eye of the storm.

PRACTICAL ADVICE
FOR PERILOUS TIMES
✦

Prof. Robert C. Smith

> *There are two ways to handle difficulties:*
> *change the situation or change yourself.*
> —ANONYMOUS
>
> *"I have told you these things,*
> *so that in me you may have peace.*
> *In this world you will have trouble.*
> *But take heart! I have overcome the world."*
> —JOHN 16:33

A cursory glance at today's news headlines confirms that we are living in perilous times. Local and national issues may temporarily crowd out news from the rest of the world, but international chaos, conflict, and crime continue to escalate. Decades of careful work to craft a lasting Middle East peace seem to collapse by the hour. The AIDS pandemic has exploded to the point where 34.3 million people worldwide are living with HIV/AIDS. According to the World Health Organization, an additional 5.4 million people were infected with HIV worldwide in the past year.

Since 1960 the United States has experienced a 560 percent increase in violent crime, a 419 percent increase in illegitimate births, a quadrupling of divorce rates, and more than a 200 percent increase in the teenage suicide rate. Christianity continues to decline in North America, while it is growing in South America, Europe, Asia, and Africa. Yes, these are perilous times . . . and the words of Paul ring true. "But mark this: There will be terrible times in the last days. People will be lovers of themselves, lovers of money, boastful, proud, abusive, disobedient to their parents, ungrateful, unholy, without love, unforgiving, slanderous, without self-control, brutal, not lovers of the good, treacherous, rash, conceited, lovers of pleasure rather than lovers of God—having a form of godliness but denying its power" (2 Tim. 3:1–5).

People react differently to the prospect that we are about to enter the last days. Some believe the best way to respond is to escape from the world and all its pressures. Since the world is going from bad to worse, they say, we ought to disengage, isolate ourselves, and look for ways to wait out the coming doom in safety. Others respond by denial. Like the proverbial ostrich, they hide their heads in the sand, deny that the last days could even be near, and then pretend the problems will go away. They live their lives with a total disregard for the future . . . and ill prepared for the times to come.

The Bible teaches that both of these responses are incorrect. In His prayer in John 17:15 Jesus did not ask God to help His followers escape from the perils of the day. Rather He prayed that His followers would be protected from the Evil One. The Scriptures instruct us not to be ignorant about the perils to come. Jesus rebuked the religious leaders of His day for such ignorance. He told them that if they could forecast the weather by looking at the meteorological signs, they should also have been able to interpret the "signs of the times" (Matt. 16:3). God expects us to examine the troubles of our day in light of His Word and to prepare ourselves for what the future holds.

God's Word provides hope for everyone facing perilous times. The Lord does not want us to be ignorant about the things to come (1 Thess. 4:13; Rev. 4:1). In fact, God revealed truth about the future to encourage us to enter into a deeper relationship with Him. It is no accident that the book of Revelation ends with an invitation to eternal life. "The Spirit and the bride say, 'Come!' And let him who hears say, 'Come!' Whoever is thirsty, let him come; and whoever wishes, let him take the free gift of the water of life" (22:17).

PRACTICAL ADVICE TO THE FOLLOWER OF JESUS IN THESE PERILOUS TIMES

A follower of Jesus Christ is someone who has turned away from a self-centered lifestyle that rejects the Word and will of God and who, by faith, trusts God for forgiveness and salvation. This results in a personal, conscious, dynamic relationship with God through Jesus Christ. More will be said about this relationship later.

For followers of Jesus Christ to cope successfully with the perils of the present age, they must first understand they need not fear the outcome. Though we should expect trials and heartaches (1 Thess. 3:1–4), we look beyond the current crisis to Christ's return for His church (4:13–18). And we also have the assurance that, as believers in Jesus Christ, we will be spared from the coming "day of the Lord" that will be a time of worldwide judgment (5:1–11). "For God did not appoint us to suffer wrath but to receive salvation through our Lord Jesus Christ" (v. 9).

Rather than being afraid about the future, the follower of Jesus can put his or her trust in a God who is trustworthy. This reliance on God results in a life marked and sustained by the peace of God (John 14:27). Such peace is not an absence of difficulties, but rather it is God's sustaining presence during such times (Phil. 4:7). For the follower of Jesus Christ this peace is a mark of true spirituality (Gal. 5:22) and allows a believer to go through perilous times with confidence in the Prince of Peace, the sustainer of all things (Isa. 9:6; Col. 1:17).

Second, the Bible teaches that, during perilous times, followers of Jesus need to live self-controlled, not undisciplined, lives. Some seek to divorce their faith from their conduct. They claim to follow Jesus, but their lives are characterized by the "acts of the sinful nature" (Gal. 5:19–21). As society moves from bad to worse, followers of Christ need to "prepare your minds for action; be self-controlled; set your hope fully on the grace to be given you when Jesus Christ is revealed" (1 Pet. 1:13).

After describing the "terrible times in the last days" (2 Tim. 3:1), the apostle Paul shared the importance of God's Word in helping believers live disciplined lives. The Word of God provides followers of Jesus Christ everything they need for "teaching, rebuking, correcting and training in righteousness, so that the man of God may be thoroughly equipped for every good work" (vv. 16–17). God uses the Scriptures to help believers handle their daily hardships.

Third, followers of Jesus need to be active in local church ministry during perilous times. As we move into a post-Christian culture, believers will need to make a conscious effort to stay attached to the one entity that will nourish them spiritually. In

1900, there was one church for every 370 people. Today there is one church for every 850 people. Approximately 3,650 churches in the United States close their doors each year. Local church attendance is just not that important today in America. But the writer of Hebrews stated the significance of church attendance for believers as the end times approach. "And let us consider how we may spur one another on toward love and good deeds. Let us not give up meeting together, as some are in the habit of doing, but let us encourage one another—and all the more as you see the Day approaching" (Heb. 10:24–25).

Two important things are to take place in the local church that cannot be done as effectively on one's own. It is hard for an individual to spur himself or herself on to love and good deeds. But when the people of God meet together in local congregations, they are able to demonstrate Christian love as they care for those in need.

Fourth, followers of Jesus Christ need to see perilous times as an opportunity to share the good news of Jesus Christ with those who have never heard. According to Wycliffe Bible Translators there are over 3,000 people groups, more than 380 million people, who still do not have the Bible translated into their language. There are still several places in the world that are closed to missionary activity and the preaching of the gospel. Many places in the world that were open to missionary activity are now becoming more hostile to the teachings of Jesus Christ. Persecution of Christians is on the increase in many nations of the world. Even the United States is experiencing a decline in its receptivity to the gospel of Jesus Christ. And yet, many of those opposed to the gospel are grasping for answers for tomorrow. They want to know what the future holds. In sharing what the Bible says about the future, we can also share the good news about Jesus Christ—the person around whom the future revolves.

Understanding the need for the sharing of the gospel worldwide, the followers of Jesus Christ need to renew their commitment to evangelism in these perilous times. Jesus told us, "As long as it is day, we must do the work of him who sent me. Night is coming, when no one can work" (John 9:4). The night is coming; the end is nearer than before. We must introduce others to Jesus Christ while we still have the opportunity.

But all of the above assumes that you know Jesus Christ as your personal Savior. What if you are *not* a follower of Jesus? Perhaps you received this book as a gift from a friend . . . or purchased it at a store because *you* have questions about the future. What practical advice does the Bible give to you if you do not have a personal relationship with Jesus Christ?

PRACTICAL ADVICE TO THOSE
WHO MAY NOT KNOW JESUS PERSONALLY

When I first became a follower of Jesus Christ as a teenager, I decided to read through the whole Bible from cover to cover and to write a short commentary on everything I had read. In fact, my commentary was to be only one sentence long! After weeks of thought and research, I reduced my understanding of the Bible to four words: *God is an extremist!*

Before you discount my statement as being too brief and simple, think about it. When God was creating the universe, He could have put just one star in the sky so that we would be struck by its unique beauty. But instead God placed billions and billions of stars in the sky . . . a number so vast that they cannot yet be counted. When we look into the sky, we are overwhelmed by the awesome greatness of a God who could create and sustain so many stars. *God is an extremist!*

Now look in the mirror and think about the uniqueness of your own physical body with its bones, circulatory system, and muscles. Think about how your brain controls this sophisticated body. No computer has been built that is as complex or efficient as a single human brain. If you were the only person on the earth, you could look at your reflection in the mirror every day and come to the awesome conclusion that only God could have made someone that complex and unique. But there are several billion people who make planet Earth their home. They come in all colors, shapes, and sizes; they speak thousands of unique languages; and they represent a vast number of different cultures. They all share the same basic genetic makeup . . . but they are all uniquely different. When we look at the human race, we can only come to one conclusion: *God is an extremist!*

To understand Bible prophecy—to grasp properly all the events in God's end-time drama—you must understand that the God who controls history and the events of humanity is an extremist. And His love, and grace, His mercy for humanity is also extreme. Therefore, if you are not a follower of Jesus, realize that this extreme God has orchestrated all of human history so that you could enter into a personal, conscious, dynamic relationship with Jesus Christ.

Human history, and your personal history, is not random or haphazard. The very fact that you grew up in the family you did, and have the language and culture you have, and live in the neighborhood you do, and are reading this book, have all been orchestrated by God Himself. He actively worked out these events in your life so that you may be inclined to turn to Him. The apostle Paul described God's awesome plan. "From one man [God] made every nation of men, that they should inhabit the whole earth; and he determined the times set for them and the exact places where they should live. God did this so that men would seek him and perhaps reach out for him and find him, though he is not far from each one of us" (Acts 17:26–27). God is actively involved in setting the times, places, and parameters of our existence. And He does this so that each and every person may have an opportunity to have a personal relationship with His Son, Jesus Christ.

The fact that you received this book and have read it to this point is not an accident. The God who placed the planets and stars in space is actively involved in your life. Why would God do this? Because He is an extremist and has used extreme measures to reach out to you.

But if God has gone through all these extreme measures to enter into a relationship with you, how should you respond? God's Word says that you should repent of your sin and self-centeredness . . . and turn to God for forgiveness and salvation. Sin at its core is rebellion against God's control of our lives for the purpose of living a self-centered life. And sin has infected—and affected—the whole human race (Rom. 3:23).

God knew that humanity would be totally incapable of dealing with its sin problem. That is why God provided the means of overcoming sin by sending His one and only Son, Jesus Christ, to pay the price for our sin, setting us free from its grip once and for all. The Scriptures speak of the fact that Jesus had to die to pay the price of our sin.

"God made him who had no sin to be sin for us, so that in him we might become the righteousness of God" (2 Cor. 5:21).

"He himself bore our sins in his body on the tree, so that we might die to sins and live for righteousness; by his wounds you have been healed" (1 Pet. 2:24).

"Christ was sacrificed once to take away the sins of many people; and he will appear a second time, not to bear sin, but to bring salvation to those who are waiting for him" (Heb. 9:28).

If you are going to make it through perilous times, especially those perilous times you have brought on yourself because of your sin, you will need to repent and ask God to wash away all your sin and cleanse you from all your guilt (Ps. 51:2).

This act of repentance is the beginning of a process that ends with a personal, conscious, and dynamic relationship with Jesus as Savior and Lord. Maybe this is the first time you have considered your eternal destiny, or maybe the burden of sin is so overwhelming that you can bear it no more, or maybe the perilous times you are going through have robbed you of a future and a hope. Then I have good news for you—the extremist God has extreme love, mercy, forgiveness, and redemption for you. All you need to do is to follow four simple steps to turn toward God and trust Him . . . and He will meet you where you are.

Step 1—Acknowledge the fact that you are a sinner. "For all have sinned and fall short of the glory of God" (Rom. 3:23).

Step 2—Realize that God is both just and loving, and that He is extreme in His justice and love. He is a just God who must punish sin. "For the wages of sin is death" (Rom. 6:23). "The LORD is slow to anger and great in power; the LORD will not leave the guilty unpunished" (Nah. 1:3). But He does love you and is willing to forgive you by allowing His Son to pay the penalty for your sin. "But God demonstrates his own love for us in this: While we were still sinners, Christ died for us" (Rom. 5:8).

Step 3—Believe that Jesus Christ took your place of punishment on the cross and died there to pay the ultimate price for your sin. His physical resurrection from the dead confirmed that His sacrificial death was acceptable to God.

Step 4—Understand that eternal life can be yours by simple faith in Jesus Christ. All you need to do is to place your trust in Jesus. "For God so loved the world that he gave his one and only Son, that whoever believes in him shall not perish but have eternal life" (John 3:16).

You can take these four basic steps by pausing right now and praying to God. The following is a simple prayer you can pray.

"Dear Lord Jesus, I know I am a sinner and need Your forgiveness. I believe that You died for my sins on the cross. I want to turn from my sins. I now invite You into my heart to forgive me and give me eternal life. I want to trust You as my Savior. Amen."

Understand that merely mouthing a prayer does not automatically make you a follower of Jesus Christ. The real issue has to do with what happens in your heart at a spiritual level. But if you mean these words in your heart as you pray them, then you have indeed had your sins forgiven, received eternal life, become a follower of Jesus Christ, and entered into a new relationship with Him. Why not tell a Christian friend or pastor about your decision? I am sure they will want to help you develop in your relationship with Jesus. It is very important at this early stage of your spiritual development to enlist the help of other Christians in your personal growth.

Every day seems to bring the world closer to the "last days" and the "perilous times" that are said to accompany them. Before these days finally come crashing down, God has promised to take His children home to heaven. As followers of Jesus, we need to realize that our summons to come home could come at any moment. Now is not the time to get discouraged or to "throw in the towel." Instead, this is the time when our light for God should shine the brightest in a dark and needy world.

And for those who have not yet come to know Christ personally, what are you waiting for? Jesus is still calling you to come to Him . . . to enter into a relationship with Him as Savior and Lord. But time is running out. Jesus said at the end of the book of Revelation, "Yes, I am coming soon" (Rev. 22:20). Yesterday has passed. Tomorrow is uncertain. Today may be your final opportunity to trust in Him as your Savior. Don't delay. "For he says, 'In the time of my favor I heard you, and in the day of salvation I helped you.' I tell you, now is the time of God's favor, now is the day of salvation" (2 Cor. 6:2).